A SURVIVOR MYSELF

EXPERIENCES OF CHILD ABUSE

EDITED BY
PAULINE KIRK

Everyone has a story
to tell. We find
ways of helping
them tell it.

YORKSHIRE ART CIRCUS
1994

Published by Yorkshire A
School Lane, Glasshough
West Yorkshire, WF10 4Q]
Telephone (0977) 550401

Production: Reini Schühle, Ian Daley, Olive Fowler,
Fiona Edwards, Linda Smith
Typesetting: Ian Daley, Art Circus Education
Printer: FM Repro, Roberttown, Liversedge

ISBN 1 898311 02 1
Classification: Social Sciences

Yorkshire Art Circus is a unique book publisher. We work to
increase access to writing and publishing and to develop new
models of practice for arts in the community.
Please write to us for details of our full programme of
workshops and our current book list.

Yorkshire Art Circus is a registered charity No 1007443

Yorkshire Art Circus is supported by:

CONTENTS

FOREWORD
By Jane M Wynn
Consultant Community Paediatrician, Leeds

As a paediatrician, albeit with an interest in all forms of child maltreatment, it may be unexpected that the editor should ask me to write this foreword. Having read the book, the connection is clear: all the authors suffered as children and we, the adult world, didn't see or hear their distress. They were labelled bad, delinquent or disturbed but no one seems to have listened to them or wondered why?

The points are well made: abuse occurs at home, school and in residential units. Boys as well as girls are abused. Abuse may involve the very young. It occurs in all social classes and ethnic groups. The abuse may be institutionalised. Racism is an additional form of emotional abuse and may involve physical violence. Whilst abused children need not become abusing adults, parents who were abused themselves may not be able to protect their children from inter-generational abuse. Parents with mental health problems, including addiction, need help - but so do the children.

All the authors have been emotionally harmed and have invariably suffered through sexual and physical abuse and neglect. As adults all have struggled in forming relationships with other adults.

Whilst this a sad book, survival is possible and I think if this book is widely read by victims of abuse, it will give hope to those who are ready to hear. But it should also be read by all professionals working with children: Much of our understanding of child abuse has been learned from survivors and this book adds to that knowledge.

Finally there is optimism as victims become survivors, accepting that their abusive experience is managed - there is no "cure", but after considerable turmoil the reader does recognise their successes.

4

INTRODUCTION
by Pauline Kirk

A book about survivors of child abuse could be very depressing. When I started to edit this collection, I feared I might find the next few months harrowing. Instead, I have found the experience unexpectedly uplifting.

Many of the survivors who tell their stories here, have overcome appalling disadvantages, and have gone on to achieve a great deal. Even those who are still struggling to come to terms with their memories show a courage and tenacity which I can only admire.

From the start, I decided to include men as well as women. In my work for Social Services, I have gained the impression that there is a danger of child abuse being seen as only affecting women and girls. That is unfair to the men and boys who have suffered - and are still suffering - abuse. I also have a sneaking suspicion that if men see the issue as affecting them too, rather than just as 'a women's problem', more might be done about it.

Finding groups which assist child abuse survivors was not a problem, though obtaining up-to-date addresses and contacts proved difficult. There are a growing number of groups, many listed in the Directory at the end of this book. Understandably however, both those who work with survivors and survivors themselves are suspicious of outsiders. They have had unfortunate experiences of having their stories sensationalised. It took me some months to gain people's confidence.

Once I had done so, I found eleven survivors - five men and six women - who were willing to talk to me. Some of these were already finding that writing about their childhood helped them to come to terms with their experiences, and I have included extracts from their autobiographies and poems here. Others I talked to over several weeks, carefully noting what they told me, and then sending the drafts of their piece to them for approval. Where requested, names and places may have been changed to protect the speaker, but nothing else has been altered. I was lucky in finding eleven people who can talk so eloquently about a distressing subject. By the end of the book, I hope the reader will have come to share my respect for those without whose help this book would not have been possible.

Lessons from Mr Biggs

Joe was born in Yorkshire, and is a professional writer. He is becoming quite well known, and few of his readers would suspect the unpleasant memories which he carries from his childhood.

At the age of seven Joe was abused by a school teacher. Like many abused children he found great difficulty telling adults what was happening.

Witnessing two road accidents at about the same time increased his distress. Blurring into his recollections of abuse, these half-understood incidents gave him a sense of vague nightmare which stayed with him for years.

Two years ago Joe began writing about his childhood. He says the story which follows 'was begun in a fairly aimless and unfocussed way, when it dawned on me that I could use that bad experience to explain or excuse some of my past behaviour.'

Since then, Joe has found writing about his memories is one way of coming to terms with the experience of abuse. He can now tell his story with wit, and even humour.

With the carrot and stick combination of Mr Biggs' caressing my genitals and Dad's impatient tutoring, I was a fairly advanced reader by the age of seven. Mr Biggs wasn't my teacher, but he took a shine to me and literally held me up in front of his class of nine year olds, where I would precociously demolish the book they were stammering through. I didn't realise that I was earning the undying scorn of those children, although I was aware that what Mr Biggs was doing out of their sight, with his hand ventriloquist-style up the back of my shorts, was probably wrong.

It didn't matter too much because I wasn't averse to the sensations. Anyway, he liked me, ruffled my hair and kissed me like my Dad did. When I moved on to a new book his hand moved on in congratulatory style making me feel my head was exploding. I didn't know my arse from my elbow but Mr Biggs did. My thoughts about it all were along the lines of, 'Why does he want to put his fingers into places I've been taught are dirty? And if it's dirty why does it feel so good?'

Every lunchtime I'd wander through to his empty classroom in a state of semi-arousal, jump on his knee and open whichever book I was on. He'd munch his sandwiches, making fond noises whilst interfering with me using his free hand. That arrangement worked well for about three months until one day he requested that I did the same for him.

Panic - I was trapped. The idea of putting my hand on what was poking through his flyhole made me feel sick. But if I didn't do anything, he wouldn't be my friend. Fear of his smelly dick made me bolt for the door. It had shrivelled fearfully into his trousers by the time he caught me. I don't recall what he said exactly, but it was a mixture of cajoling and threats along the lines that we'd both be in for real big trouble if ever I told anybody.

I kept out of his way after that. Whenever he saw me, he'd put a finger to his lips that only looked like a teacher shushing kids to anyone else. Monsters lurked around every corner of my mind. Instead of trotting off to see Mr Biggs, I skulked around the cloakroom hiding under coats. Then, when nobody came looking for me, I rifled through pockets and wandered to the forbidden shop with my booty where I stuffed myself with as many sweets as I could afford. After that I'd either sit on the school wall overlooking the main road waving my willie at the passing traffic, or wee on the altar in the church dominating our playground, whose walls were so sacred that God saw every rubber ball bouncing off them.

Unforced, real life had compounded my disturbed nature during the year that Mr Biggs was interfering with me. Up until six years ago, I'd assumed that what follows was a vivid, ineradicable childish nightmare.

One sunny spring afternoon we had a family day out at a reservoir in the Pennines. Dad's friend Bert was scuba diving which was only exciting when a black rubber head broke the water unexpectedly, so I had my back to the reservoir and eyes only for the main road where a parade of interesting cars was passing. I saw the red Bubble Car coming down that moorland road going really fast. Then its single wheel began skipping like I'd never seen before until it took off, and the car began rolling back-over-front straight down the middle of the road directly in front of me. A woman in a 1963, belted summer dress popped from the somersaulting car and bounced for a long time down the road. In my childish self-absorption I thought it was my fault.

That woman's image haunted me for years. I was thirty before I asked my parents whether or not it had really happened. They exchanged resigned expressions, like I was finally old enough to have it confirmed. I'm not sure though, why they were surprised at me remembering.

I began wetting my trousers shamefully often, then sitting miserably through lessons dressed in my dufflecoat, short trousers steaming accusingly at me from the radiator. Mr King, the headmaster, called in the educational psychologist after I'd briefly aroused the sympathy of the entire school by arriving one morning and announcing tearfully that my mum had just been killed in a bus crash. When Mum called from beyond the grave to pick me up that day and heard the long list of what I'd been up to, she could only agree with Mr King about the need for outside help.

I wasn't the only weirdo at St Michael's, because the day they came to do the tests, my classmate Mick was

9

there too. It was a hopeful spring afternoon. The psychologist was a pretty, kind woman who soon had me and Mick laughing. There was a health visitor too. It was she who instructed us both to strip down to our underpants and vests. Panicking, I deployed delaying tactics.

'I need to go to the toilet.'

'Very well, slip off your trousers and run along then,' she instructed.

'I need to go too,' said Mick.

So we both raced to the toilets in the playground and the kids in class stood up at the windows, shrieking as me and Mick streaked past in our underpants. Alerted by the unusual sound of happy kids, Mr O'Neil, the deputy head, appeared at his office window and roared at us. Two pairs of plastic sandals slewed to a halt.

Mr O'Neil poked his head through his pokey window. 'I might have known!' he barked. 'The two most stupid, ridiculous boys in the entire school have finally teamed up.' We stood grinning - we belonged to a higher authority than him and we knew it. 'Wipe those ridiculous expressions off your faces this minute. What in God's name do you think you're doing?'

So we told him, and he shook his head like he was sad as he closed his windows.

Despite my doing well in the tests, the headmaster told Mum that I was 'ineducable'. Luckily Mrs Barker, my teacher, liked me. 'Always remember,' she used to say, 'education is what they take out of your head, not what they put in.'

Eventually Mr Biggs' constant but surreptitious warnings to keep quiet worked against him. After a lot of nightmares and worrying, I worked out that if there was going to be trouble, it was better I got my side of the story in first. It took a long time plucking up the courage, but one Saturday morning I seated myself opposite Dad, whose entire upper body was hidden by the *Daily*

Telegraph he was reading. That was good. I didn't want to see his face. I knew exactly how to do it. I'd rehearsed it in my mind for weeks so I remember the exchange well.

Straight-forwardness was the only approach Mum or Dad would dignify with an audience.

'Dad - '

'Hmm,' he grunted without lowering the newspaper.

'Mr Biggs puts his fingers up my bottom.'

The newspaper came crashing down far too quickly, for the casual manner he later employed to interrogate me, ever to be convincing.

'Maureen!'

Mum, drying her hands on a tea towel, came in quickly, alerted by the odd note in Dad's tone.

'Tell your mother what you've just told me.'

They both stared as I squirmed.

'Mr Biggs puts his finger up my bottom and plays with my willie and kisses me,' I blurted.

After that I was taken down to the police station, where I refused to add anything more. I felt like a dirty, mortal sinner. The detective interviewing me wasn't like the ones I'd seen on *Z-Cars*. 'You just tell me what he did to you Sonny, and I'll show you where we keep prisoners,' was his approach. But I stayed quiet, knowing for certain it was the big trouble Mr Biggs had warned me about. I remember playing with the Corgi Mini Cooper my dad had just bought me; wheeling it, with my head down, on a flat table and evading their questions.

I didn't let the copper know anything I hadn't told my Mum and Dad. Telling my parents had taken a big weight from me but there was nobody to talk about it with. Mum and Dad went into a period of denial which thirty years later has become unbreachable. For years I thought there was something wrong with me because of what Biggs did.

He was never seen at St Michael's again, yet curiously

he was never prosecuted. My credibility as a witness had probably been ruined when the story about Mum's fatal accident was seen as evidence of my untrustworthiness, rather than as a symptom of sexual abuse.

I don't think Mr Biggs went beyond what I remember, but you don't have to bugger someone to start buggering them up. There was no doubt that I was disturbed but I was never trapped in the same household as my abuser, like some kids.

I could go on to relate my criminal adolescence, but the further away I move from the childhood abuse and guilt, the more tenuous the link between that and my behaviour becomes. When Mum and Dad moved me from St Michael's to another school, my childhood seemed to pass happily enough.

When I lived in the north, as the father of one-and-a-half children, I attended a seminar on child abuse. The woman in charge was skilled at getting children to open up about their experiences. She showed us a video of herself in action with a young girl, using dolls and other toys to draw out and gain the trust of the child. So much patience, sensitivity and subtlety needed. I thought back to my dad and that copper.

'Many abused children become abusers themselves in adult life,' I heard her say. So I got angry.

'I've never wanted to abuse any child... It doesn't necessarily follow...'

But all my life I've abused, usually verbally like when I tore into her, and often with fists to back up my wicked mouth. Never with kids though, just in case you're thinking the worst. But arguing my case rationally is something I still find impossible.

Everything's personal with me. I was thirty-three before I managed to go twelve months without having to physically fight. A psychiatrist friend who didn't then know my full story, laughed Stephen Fry style, when I told him I wanted to change. I wanted to smash him in his smug gob, but I didn't. I've got a problem with authority figures. I'm too much like my dad these days.

Analysing my behaviour over the thirty years since Biggs sexually abused me is a bit like chicken and egg. Constantly speculating over whether my low self-esteem is down to Biggs' treatment of me as a small child, or my own subsequent pattern of self-defeating behaviour, now seems to me a nebulous quest. Analysis has an ironic ring to it in the light of where Biggs was putting his fingers. Constantly peer up your own back passage and all you'll ever see is darkness. I'm not saying you shouldn't look honestly at what disturbed you, but don't let it horror you into paralysis.

I don't feel that what I underwent at the hands of Biggs was damaging enough to now merit calling me a survivor. During the years he was molesting me, I witnessed the Bubble Car incident, two boys spilling from the backs of moving cars and another boy bouncing off the bonnet of a Hillman Minx. Recalling those incidents is more traumatic to me than memories of what Biggs did.

I'm a happy man these days. I'm married to a beautiful woman and have two lovely children. Apart from a brief androgynous period inspired by David Bowie during puberty, I've enjoyed a healthy libidinous heterosexual life. Writing about what happened to me has been therapeutic and if the ghost of Biggs isn't entirely banished, he doesn't cast the same shadow as he once did.

Ssh Ssh Baby

Shirley was born in Basseterre, St Kitts, of a Kittitian mother and Anguillan father. Her mother left for England when Shirley was very young, and she was looked after by her godmother ('Mama') and an older cousin, Miss Cranston or 'Mummy'.

In September 1963, Shirley and Mummy left for England. By the following February Mummy was dead. Shirley was left stranded in England and was fostered by Miss Cranston's daughter. For nearly ten years she suffered physical, emotional, and sexual abuse in her foster home, until in May 1972 she ran away, two weeks before taking her 'A' Levels.

Since then, Shirley has achieved a great deal, gaining qualifications in Needlecraft and Design and Social Studies. Her first post was in a Comprehensive School, then as a peripatetic teacher working for a language school; she taught English as a second language. Following a short period in London she returned to Birmingham to establish Nefertiti Arts and Crafts.

The founder and co-ordinator of Burbury Creative Writers' Circle, Shirley was also an Executive Member of the Federation of Worker Writers and Community Publishers. She is heavily involved in Afro-Caribbean, Community and Women's groups in the Birmingham area, and 'founded, co-founded, spearheaded, pioneered (sometimes without funding), groups dating back to the early 1970s.' One of these, W.A.V.E.S. - Women Against Violence Engaging in Support - provides regular meetings for survivors of domestic violence.

In her poems and stories Shirley frequently draws on the patois of her childhood. ' will not apologise for the language used,' she says. 'As a child I spoke a variety of patois (creole or nation language) and Standard English. I do not see it as broken English, Bad

Daddy

Daddy, why you do this to me
Daddy it's wrong can't you see
Daddy you no suppose to touch me so
Daddy it isn't right you know
Daddy you can go to jail
Daddy what if dat thing you use fail
Daddy it ain't right you know
Daddy de Bible tell you so
Daddy dis is a disgrace
Daddy how you could bear to show you face
Daddy what if Mummy find out
And Uncle Len give you a clout
Daddy what if you pregnant me
Daddy it's wrong can't you see
Daddy I tell me friend today
Daddy teacher say they gon take you away
Daddy you say no play wid boys
I too old to play wid toys
Daddy you are fucking sick
Daddy I don't want to play with your dick
Daddy if you don't let go
I will let everybody know
Daddy what you doing ain't right
You ain fucking me tonight
Find someone you size to poke
Daddy dis ain't no joke
Daddy don't you think is wrong
You are very big and strong
What can I do to stop you

15

When you're nearly forty-two
Don't you think that ten's too young
to indulge in fornication
Daddy you are fucking sick
Daddy better get out quick
Forgot to tell you, on the way
Home from school I stopped to say
To the police up the street
Where Daddy want to put his meat.

I was abused from the moment of conception; perhaps during. My mother was regularly beaten up and my godmother told me about some specific occasions: when my mother was six months pregnant with me; the day I was born and at my christening less than a month later.

My father was a bully and an alcoholic. He used to beat up my mother. Finally her father sent her to England - because she had had three children and had never been married. Going to England did not change things for my mother however because she went into another violent relationship. She left me and my sisters with my godmother, Mama.

My father, Joseph, died when I was three. Mama used to tell me about him. He was one of the best mechanics in St Kitts. He used to fix motorbikes and when he had done, he would take them for a try. One other thing about him, he was always drunk. He used to come in, take the Carnation milk, and when my mother said she wanted the milk for the baby he used to point to the rum bottle and say, 'Give she dat.' So Mama said I drank rum when the rest of the babies drank milk.

I remember my father coming in and asking for me, then chasing me for a kiss. One day I hid under the bed with all the shoes, and when I was right up the corner, I saw a lizard. I wasn't sure if I was most afraid of the lizard under there or my drunken father. When Miss

Cranston got me from under the bed I cried until I couldn't cry any more.

Mama used to tell me about my father's death. Her story always went the same:

'Once upon a time Joseph get somebody motorbike to fix. When he done fix it he say to he friend, "I going to try it."'

'Joseph, you carn go ride de bike. You ha ine too much liquor.' But Joseph he big big, so he get pon the bike and went Broomm Broomm past the Gas Station, up pass the Anglican and straight through College Street Gut where Shirley born. Well Joseph feel nice and he going fast fast. De next thing we hear, Joseph round the Fort and he going so fast he see Mr Mollineaux wall coming for him. When Mr Mollineaux come out he shout, 'A who dat a mash down me wall?' When he look, Joseph dead.'

Mama used to dress us up sometimes to take us to see our grandfather on the Bay Front. He had a big shop where he sold mattresses and furniture. I used to climb up on to the top of the mattresses. Papa (our grandfather) used to make belts as well which he beat us with. When I was three, Papa took us to live with him. Mama always said it was because our mother was working and Papa wanted the money she sent.

Miss Cranston was a cousin of ours. She had one child, Eileen, who had gone to Aruba at seventeen. Miss Cranston used to come to comb our hair. She especially liked combing mine because it was nice and straight. I liked her. One day I asked her 'Wha you name?'

'What do you mean, "What's my name?" You know my name is Miss Cranston, Cousin Ruth.'

'No, you name Mummy,"'I said. 'You name Mummy,' and from that day I refused to call her anything else.

In 1958, when I was five, our real mother was found dead in England. Papa shared out her children because Mama couldn't afford to keep us. He found friends and family with money to send us to. Mummy had two houses and travelled a lot. She could afford to give me a good education. Mama reluctantly gave me up, but Miss Cranston kept returning me to her whenever she went to Aruba to see her daughter.

Attempts 'to beat the devil out of me' as a child were in vain. It didn't stop me doing what I wanted to and I ran away twice. I got beaten with anything, shoes, sticks, wire, belts.

It was normal.

In England the few attempts to beat me were futile. If the purpose was to make me cry, it didn't work because I was 'a hard yam'. The last time I got beaten at home was when I lent a blue typing book to my cousin Gwen. Months later when my grandfather sent the typewriter from St Kitts, Gwen couldn't find the book. I was beaten for lending it to her, and because I didn't cry I was never beaten by a parent again.

Mummy decided to take me to England in 1963. Some months before, Aruba had told all non-Dutch Citizens to leave. America didn't want any more immigrants and England had jobs for coloured people. Mummy told me that her daughter didn't want to come back to St Kitts. She went to England instead.

Then her daughter wrote asking Mummy to come to England as things were hard. She couldn't get a reliable child minder and her youngest child, her only boy, had drunk some poison and nearly died.

Mummy wrote back and said that if she was going to England I must come too, because she had had me since I was three. Eileen replied that she had six children and she couldn't afford to feed another one. If Mummy wanted to take me to England she had to pay for me herself.

So Mummy wrote a will and left one of her houses for me. Then she sold some of her things and packed the rest in two rooms in the side of the house. If she didn't like

England, she had three houses and her things to come back to.

The day came and the car arrived for us. As we drove down the road I felt like the Queen. I waved to everybody, but when I got to the airport and saw Mama, Papa, Medora and all the other children, I started to cry. Mama hugged me and told me I was leaving one sister to go to another. Frances had already gone to her father in Leeds 7 and I was going to Leeds 8, so we were only going to be one Leeds away. But I never believed her because Mama always said, 'If they bring England and put it in Warner Park I ain going.'

Like with the time when I ran away, I was forced onto the plane. I sat and bawled. Nothing good could happen in England. Wasn't that where my mother had died because she never liked it? I didn't see why Papa wanted me to go there because he went once himself, and came back when they gave him a broom and told him, 'You people can't be auctioneers in England.'

In no time we reached Antigua. We went shopping in the airport and I bought a book with pictures of coloured people. It was called *Ladybird Africa*. Mummy was annoyed. I didn't know it at the time, but this was the beginning of many things, including my Black Consciousness and my quest for survival using my collection of stories, *Memories from Home*.

On September 23rd we arrived in England. The date is important to me as it is also the date when I left Leeds. After St Kitts it was cold, and Mummy had arrived without a coat. She only had a thick cardigan. She fell down the stairs at her daughter's carrying a paraffin heater, and in February she died of pneumonia.

I was left with Eileen's family. The Care of Children Department came in. Mummy had told me to get my grandfather to have me back, but he replied that in England they looked after you and I should stay. If I returned to St Kitts he would have to pay. So the family said I could stay with them providing I behaved myself, and I was fostered with them.

I tried, I really tried to be perfect, but Eileen blamed me for her mother's death. I can recall her shouting and bawling at me at the funeral. Part of the problem was that Eileen was jealous of her mother bringing me up seventeen years after her. By the time Mummy had me, she had three houses and money. They weren't very nice about my own mother's death either. They kept insisting that she had committed suicide, even though the verdict was misadventure. She had died from a faulty gas fire, one of many in 1958. I've got her letters though and know how unhappy she was. It could well have been suicide.

It was thrown at me how lucky I was and how grateful I should be for living there. It was mental abuse. I was constantly made to feel unwelcome.

My foster mother didn't acknowledge she was paid £8 a week to care for me. Yet I did everything I could to please her. No matter how hard I tried, I never did anything right for her. I was the best cook in the house and cooked dinner for the whole family on Sundays. After school there was no food. I was not fed for days on end. Someone stole my pocket money. Social Services sent money every week for me, and I had to pay for my music lessons, bus fares and sanitary towels out of that 2/6 per week. I told the woman from Social Services but she did bugger all. Instead of telling my foster mother the 2/6 was for me, Social Services just increased the money and she kept it just the same.

I used to think I was first sexually abused when I was fourteen. It was a bonfire night and I went upstairs to get changed, and my foster father came into the room and rubbed himself against me. Since then I have a 'thing' about November the Fifth. But I realised one day that I had a particular dress on during one incident. I posed for a photograph in that dress and always thought it was strange that I was eleven and the number in the photograph was eleven. Therefore I was eleven when the incident happened.

During my daughter's tenth year though I was particularly edgy. Whilst rubbing her down during an illness, I had a flashback of my foster father rubbing me down within weeks of me coming to England. Again it was near a bonfire night. I had been in England about six weeks. I remember thinking his hand should not have been there. I can recall the room and the position of the bed, and see him leaning over me.

I realise now my foster father saw my situation and took advantage of it. Even before Mummy's death he started putting his hand round me on the sofa.

He used to tell me dirty jokes and show me photographs: one of a naked man fishing, and other pornographic ones. Another showed a school girl having oral and vaginal sex with two men. I stole the photos and showed them to my sister. She asked me where I got them and tore them up.

In the early years he was content with fingering. He always made a point of sitting next to me on the settee in the dark. As I grew older he went further and further. He told me to wash myself properly after he'd 'played' with me. I spent long periods in the bathroom, usually washing in cold water. There was no pleasure without pain, he said. If I struggled I would only hurt my insides.

Soon he was into oral sex. Then he tried penetration. He and his wife were not living together. They had separate rooms and he lived in the attic next door to me and one of his daughters. His wife sent me to buy Ortho Gynol vaginal cream, and I remember reading the box on my way through the park from Chapeltown Road. He kept it in his room and used it on me.

Whenever he realised I was alone in our room he would come in. He used to say, 'Let's us two unwanteds get together.' He called me 'Ssh! Ssh!'

He spent a lot of time in his bed and kept food on a little table across the room. He would call me in and ask me to get something off the table for him. When I handed it to him he would grab my hand. If I refused I was rude and he was going to put me in a Home.

My foster mother, after a man in the area had made his stepdaughter pregnant, commented that nobody could tell her the husband interfered with them, because they must want it. The way she discussed the abused girl, I realised I couldn't tell her anything. Besides, seeing how I was being mistreated I doubt if I would have tried making a complaint.

I feel she knew what was happening. She sent me for the contraceptive cream after all. Now I've done so much work on domestic violence I realise it may have eased the pressure on her. She may not have been in a position to do anything about it. I'm sure one or two of the other girls staying in the house were abused by him. Maybe my foster mother felt it was better to have him using me rather than one of his own daughters.

There were positive sides to the abuse because he would tempt me with food, which I wasn't getting. He took me on walks with him, sometimes to the launderette and then on to the swimming baths while the clothes were washing. It was 'our secret'. At times he bought me presents. A birthday card I remember once said, 'Only open this card if you can face reality.' Inside was the capitalised word REALITY. He then showed me his reality - his penis. Another time he bought me a branded pair of tights and wanted to see me put them on.

I went to grammar school, one of six Black children there. I was popular; the comic, cheeky, reliable, the most daring. It was not too good a time for me although I had caring teachers. I had all the signs of an abused child but no one recognised them. There was blood on my clothes from me scratching my arms all the time; I played truant, went to school in dirty clothes. My school reports never said anything about me being absent so much. Maybe some teachers did recognise the signs but didn't know what to do.

I used to be very sickly and after a while I used to go to school with bronchitis and period pains rather than stay alone with him. One day I actually went to school in the afternoon and cried in the classroom. I failed my 'O' Levels because I couldn't stay in the house to revise. I did most of it in the park. I was safer in an empty park during the day than in the house. Before the next lot of exams I didn't tell anyone that we had time off for revision. I got up every day, got dressed, left the house at the right time and spent the day in the library or museum.

I saw a Perry Mason show once where the girl got raped. When they found her she was singing a nursery rhyme. She had sung it all the way through the rape. I used to think of the Caribbean: the day when I was going to go back there with Mama and live happily ever after. That's probably why Joan Riley's *The Unbelonging* feels like my story.

I developed other survival techniques. My first nine years in St Kitts prepared me for the nine in Leeds. I wrote on every piece of paper I could find, made up stories, drew, and kept a red diary in which I wrote in code. I also read a lot: *Bunty*, *Mandy*, *Judy*, *Loving*, and spent hours searching for anything to do with my life. A lot of my time was spent in the school library.

I got comfort from Bible stories too, remembering quotes and reading the Bible I was given as a going away present in St Kitts. Songs helped, like *Sad Movies* which I heard back home, *Shoo Fly* and *Nobody's Child*. Music was important to me. Whenever I could get into the sitting room I played the piano, and listened to music on a blue transistor with earplugs. (Maybe that's why I can't stand 'Walk-a-Mans' now.) Sometimes I went next door, to an old Jamaican woman who taught us Caribbean folk songs and sayings.

I also studied hard. My foster father helped me with my homework but I could never get the grades he wanted. Even though I came second in the Twelve Plus and got a grammar school place, I should have come first!

As often as possible, I spent weekends and overnight with white school friends. Their parents looked after me, gave me presents, essentials sometimes, like warm clothes. If I could, I tried to get to Birmingham, to my uncle, but I never told him what was happening. My foster family had made me believe nobody wanted me. I didn't tell my grandfather in St Kitts either. He didn't send for me, therefore I couldn't let him know I was ungrateful to this family that had taken me in. I did write home to Mama, lots of tear stained letters which she said years later she couldn't read.

Most of the work in the house was done by me. That's how I got myself into abusive relationships later. I can see the patterns. I needed attention. The book *Women Who Love Too Much* suggests one way of getting the attention you did not get in your childhood, is having a man who wants you and needs you, so you make every excuse for him. It leads to sexual abuse as an adult also. You get into a situation where you don't particularly want to be in a sexual relationship with a man but you don't get out of it. You have an inability to say 'No' because you never had a chance to do so when you were a child. There is also the fear that the man might take it out on you, and the fear of losing him, having lost before. So you shut out, cut off. You think of something else - you 'freeze'. You learn to do that as a child and do it in adulthood. It's self-protection.

I was around seventeen when I went into my first abusive relationship. When I wasn't being verbally abused it was physical.

The 1972 Motown hit *Ain't too Proud to Beg* still brings back memories of a love affair I had at the time with a Jekyll and Hyde character. He was a new face in Chapeltown. Everyone fell for his tall dark handsome looks. He didn't speak like the other Chapeltown boys. He had come from another side of town, a posher, cleaner, middle class area. At the United Caribbean Association and at Roscoes, the Church Youth Club, everyone talked about Tony. Between Club nights the local chatter was who Tony danced with, who he walked home and who he'd made a date with. I stood aside. I wasn't interested in this new boy. I already had my future husband.

He wasn't as tall, he wasn't as handsome and he went to the local Boys' School. I went to the Grammar, therefore it wasn't long before the foster 'family' decided that he was unsuitable. In those days, 'Black wasn't beautiful'.

Finally, the strain to hang on became too much. I had either to finish the relationship or go into a Home. We decided that the Homes were in white areas and I wouldn't be able to see him at all, so it was easier to 'cool it'.

Tony meanwhile took a liking to me at a dance and asked me out. Maybe it was because I was hurting, maybe it was a challenge. I knew he had had a steady girlfriend with a child. But we all knew, as we always did in our area, that they'd finished. So we arranged a date.

I should have walked away. Being very adventurous though I went out with him. I was in love. Here was a man who took me out to nice places: Batley Variety Club, Mecca Dancing, cafes, the cinema; places where we were almost always the only black couple. He helped me to copy up my 'A' Level notes. We wrote poems together. These were my musical days. I used to play piano and sing in a group a couple of years before, and as Tony sang too, we made a good couple. Shirley and Tony were synonymous with Romeo and Juliet in more ways than one. Unlike Tony's ex girlfriend I encouraged him to pursue his musical career.

Unfortunately, Tony was wildly jealous. I mistook it for love. 'If I didn't love you, I wouldn't hit you,' he said and I believed him. We fought everywhere, at parties if someone else looked at me, on the streets, anywhere. It was rumoured all round the community. My foster family loved the suave, sweet-talking Tony. I told no one about the 'other' Tony. Every time I threatened to finish with him, he'd sing the song loud and clear: 'I know you wanna leave me, but I refuse to let you go. Ain't too proud to beg.'

Then he'd make threats.

I was told that I wasn't a woman because women don't hit back, they cry. His previous girlfriend used to cry and beg him not to hit her. At first I used to hit back. The last time I decided not to. I had just seen him kick his three year old brother across the room, and I vowed that if I stayed in that relationship and had kids for him, I would have to kill him.

Eventually, I pulled out, and Tony did beg. It was dramatic. His friends begged, my friends begged, he wouldn't do it again. I went back again and again. I was about to go back again when the previous boyfriend, having been sent details by a well-wisher, wrote and asked why I didn't finish with Tony once and for all. Securing his interests perhaps.

Finally, in May 1972 after an approach from my foster father, I made a suicide attempt. I collected every tablet in the house. It was as if somebody knocked the tablets out of my hand and they flew all over the floor. After putting them all back in the bottles, I took a few clothes and possessions and went downstairs. I said I was going to visit a friend. I decided to go somewhere where I could study. I was doing Art and Needlework 'A' Levels, but I couldn't get any work done at home. I wanted to go to Leeds Poly to do a Needlework course, but opted for Worcester because I knew no one there.

I had £5, enough to buy a suitcase. I went to Leeds Station and asked a guy for the first train out of Leeds. It was the 8.28 pm to Birmingham, the Mail Train, that stopped at every station. I phoned an Afro-Caribbean self-help organisation and arrived there at 4.00 am. I stayed with them for two weeks. Then they collected around the group and got the money together, and sent me home to finish my 'A' Levels. One of the group phoned up to say I was coming back and the family said they couldn't care a damn. She asked me when my last exam was, and advised, 'Go after that.'

The social worker had been told I had run away because I had split up with my boyfriend. She had heard the truth from me and never listened. She told me that from the last day of school I was on my own. There were no Leaving Care Schemes then.

The miscarriage I had that summer could have been from my foster father or from my boyfriend. Just before I left home, I told a member of my foster father's family, a local Black headmistress. She told me not to tell anyone. When I was looking for alternative accommodation I told a friend I didn't want to live in a house with a man, and told her too about the abuse I'd gone through for years. She repeated it to the relative, who said, 'I thought I told you not to tell anyone... You told...'

On the 23rd September 1972 I left Leeds for good, to begin a course at Worcester College of Education. At eighteen I weighed six stones two pounds, having dropped from seven stone twelve in about six weeks.

Years later I fantasised about inviting my foster father to my house, having an affair and then killing him. When he had a stroke I used to visit him and sit staring at him, willing him to remember what he'd done to me for nine years. He died just before Christmas. His daughter phoned to tell me she had some bad news and I said 'I'm

27

glad.' My aunt also phoned to tell me the bad news, and I repeated my earlier statement. I told her the whole story. She sympathised but could do nothing about it. His wife had divorced him by then and gone to Canada.

I took the day off work for the funeral. I took my daughter to school and was going to get the train to Leeds. Someone was going to pick up my baby from the nursery so I could go. Instead I went home to think it over. I was grieving, but not for the bastard who took my childhood, my innocence away. I grieved for weeks. Everyone at school sympathised. I grieved because he shouldn't have died naturally. He was blind and in a Home before he died. They always said sex made you blind! He threatened to put me in a Home if I didn't 'let' him, but he went into one before me. I used to wonder if he ever remembered what he did to me. Although I believed God must have been sleeping through my abuse, I hope He kept that bit of my foster father's memory alert.

Although I was still hurting and my health suffered, I never talked about it. Then, when I got a computer, I sat and wrote it all up. I posted a copy to my uncle in the Caribbean, and one to the Director of Social Services, Leeds. He hoped I was getting counselling. He was aware that this happened in foster families but they were taking precautions. I was a teacher, so I had done well.

The effects? Some very abusive relationships. Battered at seventeen. Suicide attempts. Sleeping with the light on. Watching TV with the light on. Looking suspiciously at the bath. I remember sitting in school and scratching my tummy and arms until I was bleeding all over. November the Fifth is taboo. So are spermicides; ill health; anyone who looks like him. I was put on librium when I failed my 'O' Levels because I 'must have been nervous.' How many more abused sixteen year olds did they put on librium? I went on the pill at seventeen. My boyfriend couldn't understand why because he wasn't touching me. By eighteen I was on sleeping, iron and vitamin pills.

Over the years I've had flashbacks which have affected me. I still dream about it. I'm not afraid to walk late at nights or walk through deserted parks. I'm more concerned about safety in the house than outside. In nine years I experienced three attacks in Leeds by strangers, and between the ages of ten and nineteen I had regular attacks on me in the house. There were physical attacks by others in the family, as well as my foster father's sexual abuse; neglect and emotional abuse, taunts, jeers.

Other effects? Being overwhelmed by events, being self-critical, too harsh on myself; self-mutilating, feeling guilty, trying to change the world, caring too much, being abused and abused by everyone; being extra cautious or devil-may-care.

I read everything on sex abuse. I still get upset when I recognise the signs. I still space out at times. I'm persistent. I will not see any child abused, regardless of the consequences. Most importantly, I speak out so that others can speak out. Having had the strength to get out of abusive relationships, I can support other women who are experiencing domestic violence.

I have walked out with only the clothes on my back, leaving furniture, clothes etc, but coming out with as much as I can carry, and my life. I have shown my bruises. I have locked up my house and gone away from the area for days, weeks, years even. I have also done like most women, stayed and prayed and begged and cried and hoped he'd change and tried to change myself, fought back, taken the cursing and swearing and beating, cowering in the corner of the settee, freezing when he comes near. I have taken keys away and given them back. As a friend says, sometimes it's easier to open the door than have it broken down.

I've always changed my mind for those reasons or when he comes with flowers, chocolates, apologies, 'You made me do it' reasonings, 'I'll never hit you again' promises. Until the next time! Or the denials. He didn't do it. You're lying. It wasn't that bad. He loves you...

So why do we protect our men?

I can't speak for all Black women. I can speak for me. Abuse - whether sexual or physical - is a taboo subject for our community. There is this sense of loyalty we have. This urge to protect others. Who do we turn to anyway? Who do we tell? I knew what my foster father was doing was wrong but I couldn't do anything, because it would mean leaving home and going to live with white people, not having my own sort of food and losing touch with the people from outside the family I wanted to see. There was also the fact that it was secret: the threat 'You tell someone else and I'll put you in a Home.' With his wife feeling that if a girl got pregnant she must have led the man on, I couldn't tell her. There was also the whole issue of telling against a Black man to whites. Who was going to believe it any way? Even a Black headmistress told me not to tell.

I can't imagine I was bruised from head to toe by Tony and no one noticed but that's what happened. Yet attempts to talk about that too were futile. Nobody wanted to know. It was my fault. As friends and others round me were being beaten at home and hit by boyfriends, it was normal behaviour.

If you're told enough times that you are at fault you come to believe it. So you bottle it up. Blame yourself, cover up for him. Refuse to tell your doctor why you have that bruise; go to the hospital and blame the carpet you tripped on or the door that gave you that knuckle-shaped bruise. In summer you wear polo necks and in winter you wear dark glasses.

Abuse knows no barriers except sex. It cuts across race and class. The stereotyped working class, drunken man is comforting for some but not true. In conversations I'm always being asked, 'Are Black men worse?' I've never been out with a white man but my ability to read everything published that I can get hold of, and to talk to everybody, makes me believe that all things being equal, Black men are not the biggest abusers.

Over the last months my research has come up with some interesting figures. One in ten; one in four; one in three; two in three. Does anybody know the true figures? What I do know is that if all of us took action tomorrow, Legal Aid wouldn't be able to foot the bill; the few refuges would not be able to support us; and if we all hit back, the jails would not be able to hold us. Perhaps abuse ought to be renamed assault and treated as a notifiable disease.

Do you ever recover? Do you ever heal? When you have a cut, after the ointment and the plaster, don't you still bear the scar? The physical hurt might heal but what about the mental? 'Sorry can't cool it.' We said that as children in St Kitts when someone hurt us and tried to say 'Sorry'. The Bible might say, 'Forgive seventy times seven,' but it also says, 'An eye for an eye,' and 'Do unto others as you would have them do to you.' What about the little triggers, like something on the TV or radio, an article in a magazine or newspaper, seeing it happen to someone else, hearing about it, experiencing it with someone else?

I feel I have academically achieved as much as I can for now and I have to deal with those nine years, release it all and then move on. I have worked for years to cover up the hurt. As a friend always said, 'Whatever you're running away from, you'll run into it.' I can't run away from it any more, so now I'm dealing with it.

I thank God that I can write. When I came back from London and announced that I was taking up writing, a man commented that he hoped I wasn't going to be an Alice Walker. Why not? My Geography teacher used to say, 'State the obvious.' I believe I should write what I know, and if in writing about my or other people's experiences someone gets upset, tough.

So what's the answer to abuse? Publicity? Resources? A welcoming committee? Perhaps if some men thought they would find banners declaring what they had done on their front doors or cars when they woke up tomorrow, they would reconsider their actions.

I believe like Alice Walker that

because women are expected to keep silent
about their close escapes I will not keep silent.

Alice Walker also says she is

...happy to fight
all outside murderers
as I see I must.

I agree with her, but I also think we should fight all inside murderers too if we are to survive as a race.

A Quantum Shift in the Universe

Hamish is still finding his memories of sexual and physical abuse very painful. He is facing up to this pain after many years of denying it, even to himself. With the help of his family and therapist, he is now able to talk of his experiences in the family home and at boarding school, and the effect these have had on him in adulthood.

He says however, 'It is not just a matter of talking about what happened, but of coming to terms with yourself. For years you live behind a façade, and once you start to break that and try to find out who you really are, the process can't be stopped however distressing you may find it. Sometimes you want to give up and a conflict develops; part of you wants to know who you are, and the other is afraid to do so. I still don't have confidence in myself, but quite a bit of progress has been made. This has been mainly because of my wife's support. I owe her so much.'

It carried on for quite a while and started in the family home. My mother and father met in Scotland and they came down here to live. Father was born in Lincolnshire of a half Scottish mother who hated the Scots and married a man she was glad to see die - my grandad. He was very ruthless. Grandmother by contrast was very fastidious. She died in 1980, one month off a hundred, very much the Victorian. She didn't think much of children in general. Grandad killed her dog because it got covered in cow muck and she was too fastidious to clean it herself. He just wrung its neck.

We all lived together in the same house. Sometimes my grandfather was left in charge of me. On one occasion - I think it was probably the first - he gave me some drink and got me to do things to him. You see, my mother was outnumbered in the house and couldn't do anything to stop it. Grandad did some things to me as well and there were terrible arguments. If my mother tried to comfort me my grandfather would say things like, 'He needs a titty bottle again' and more crude things. It made life very difficult for her. Occasionally I would be sent to bed without anything to eat. She'd come up later and bring me some food and give me a cuddle.

Sometimes I would go into my parents' bed and my dad also - well... you know. I can't remember much but I used to run away from school when I started there and my mother got so angry that she packed my case and said she'd called a taxi, and I was being sent to a Home.

My uncle in Scotland was dying and we used to go up there for visits. My mother was a different person then. She was a different person outside the house. When I went there I used to sleep with my older cousins. They were a good bit older than me - one taught me to swim in the loch. None of them ever you know ... did what my grandfather and father did.

Mother died in 1982. After she'd died my father asked me to go to bed with him. I know it sounds unbelievable, but he did.

I was quite bright. When we moved out of my grandparents' house we had a house of our own in the country. I went to the village school and I did well. The headteacher there was a Mrs Hedges - Clara - and she used to have me over to her house, and talk to me quite a lot. I never told her anything. In later years she and her husband still took an interest in me. Her son tried to get me to go to work with him, but I couldn't. You see I was articulate, but I just didn't have confidence.

Then I passed the Eleven Plus and went to grammar school. I was always off ill and also refused to do my homework and had troubles with the masters. They thought I was bright however and tried to do the best for me. I can appreciate that now, but I hated the lot of them at the time. I saw an educational psychologist but that didn't really help, so my family sent me to a boarding school.

It was a disaster. I was bullied terribly. The school was attached to a college and had excellent facilities. There was an outdoor pool, and we had the use of the college's indoor pool too. The scholars were a mishmash of nations. Many were the sons of important political figures.

There were only seven of us from working class backgrounds. That was part of the problem. There were photos of sadomasochistic actions pupils could get hold of. Whether the information available influenced behaviour I don't know, but people with a sadistic turn are quite imaginative on their own. What ruled was self-interest. That has affected my political thinking ever since.

One boy was sadist to my masochist. It became like a symbiotic relationship. I haven't acknowledged that until recently with any clarity. I used to let him tie me up and do certain things to me. He'd want to hear about the things that had happened to me but he would go white and rigid if I tried to get him to talk about himself. It was like a fit. We did fight on occasions and his eyes would go right up into his head, and he would go on and on. He had almost certainly had some dreadful experience of his own in the past. I can't see how it can have been otherwise unless there was something mechanically wrong in his head. I have a gut feeling he isn't alive today.

We were under a pretty strict rule, almost terror. There were certain severe constraints on what could and couldn't be done. The Vice Head Boy was my main persecutor. I was basically his. The other boy had some rights though as my main persecutor fed off this relationship as well. There were times when I wanted him to kill me I think, and he would have, but he was too scared of the consequences if he even damaged me.

I've often thought *Tom Brown's School Days* is a euphemistic portrayal of what actually went on in boarding schools even in those days.

At a mental level I know it wasn't my fault, but that doesn't get rid of the feeling that it was. At interviews I've always given of my best - been too honest in fact - but I've always felt 'What are you doing here, anyway?'

I left boarding school with just one 'O' Level and got a job as a petrol pump attendant-cum-trainee manager. It was a country area and lots of people had accounts. I got the sack because I kept forgetting to put down the petrol they'd bought.

After that I got a job with a large government body abroad. It was mainly a male environment. I was sort of singled out for attention - advances, whatever.

Finally I was seduced by another man my age. It seemed like we could develop a real relationship. For the first time in my life it seemed somebody actually really wanted me. And then he was posted elsewhere. There are certain people who home in on people like me, and I just couldn't stand it again. I lasted about a fortnight then one day I was going to play hockey for the establishment. This had been arranged in advance. I went on a drinking binge just before, with nothing in my stomach. I flattened myself. I was running about the pitch and my eyesight just went. I had some peripheral vision but that was all.

They examined me in hospital and said there was nothing physically wrong, so I was sent to a psychiatric unit. The specialist there sent me back to work. I was quite suicidal by then. I went to see the doctor and said, 'If I have to stay here, I'm going to kill myself.' So I was sent to a psychiatric hospital, and had to leave work.

I didn't have many skills, and after I had recovered, I couldn't get another job. I went on a government training scheme but couldn't grasp it and ended up with a spell in a mental hospital again. They said I had a personality defect. So I came out and after several dead end jobs, I got something steady. I kept it for quite a while.

I'd always drunk quite a lot, from when I was quite young and used to go round the bars in Scotland, where they would serve you even if you were under age. Sometimes I would have a panic attack and drink to get over it. I've ridden my motorbike in some pretty dreadful states.

Two or three doors away from me there was a lad I befriended. He was a bit younger than me but his mother had died and his father had got a girlfriend and didn't want him, and had dumped him a lot on his gran and grandad. We used to talk a lot and I was pretty good on my motorbike. I had good reactions and sense of balance. I taught him a great deal about motorbikes and when he started work he said he wanted a bike of his own. I used to go around with a guy - ride in his sidecar. In a small way he was a dealer. I saw this bike he had in racing trim and asked him to save it for Phil.

Phil hadn't any experience of bikes other than what I had taught him, so I asked for the bike to be put into a state suitable for him. When I took Phil over after a week however, the bike was still in full racing trim, and the guy wouldn't alter it.

Phil was killed on that bike. People say, 'Don't blame yourself,' but deep down I don't feel anything other than blame. I don't know whether I've lacked the courage or I'm just incompetent, but I've tried to kill myself several times since his death, and failed.

Eventually, with the help of a good friend I sort of turned a corner. I met this guy because of Phil's death. He was a philosopher and I started going to his evening classes. He got me interested in getting fit and knocking the drink down a bit. I started doing judo and found I could actually do things. I could see jobs through and did quite well. I began to feel more and more confident, and even took up scuba diving. I found I was very good at it, and really thought I was going to get somewhere.

I'd never really considered relating to girls at all. They weren't part of my scheme of things, though I did have a friendship with one girl while I was working abroad. A lad I'd known as an apprentice was still friendly with me. He had a girlfriend and they'd split up. I tried to get them back together and I found myself almost unwittingly with this girl myself. She's now my wife. The most successful thing that's ever happened to me is that I've married Jill and have two kids, both doing really well for themselves.

There was a sort of unwritten agreement that the family house would be mine and my wife's ultimately, to see we were comfortable in our own old age. My father died four or five years after my mother. He'd got involved with a woman the same age as my wife. It was common knowledge in the community round where he lived that this woman bled him dry and gave him certain things in return. The relationship was grotesque. She was the sort with jodhpurs, green wellies and a county accent, while my father was working class. He cut other friends out of the house altogether.

When my father was terminally ill I took him out in the car one day, and he said, 'If I left Sylvia everything, would you contest it?' I replied, 'Yes, I would.'

In the end we got half the house. I would have swapped the whole bloody lot for him to tell me he loved me. I shaved him the night before he died and he rejected me. The next day the nurse came to tell us he had died just as we arrived at the hospital. He had done it on me, just as my grandfather did it on my grandmother, cursing her with his dying breath.

I'd started to disintegrate myself by then. I'd taken a degree in Philosophy after I'd married, and a teaching qualification. I'd thought I was going somewhere, but I hadn't been able to get a teaching post. In the end, I'd wound up back in my old firm, with a job that was very responsible but had no authority. I was going into work very early in the morning and leaving late at night, and drinking at lunch time. I was getting quite nasty with the stress and in the end I was medically retired.

When I was rejected yet again, I felt like there was nowhere for me to go, that I was finished. If I killed myself, it would play havoc with my two kids and my wife. I couldn't do it. It was like being two people. One wanted to go on and do things. And the other - well, it wanted pain and death.

My marriage started to go to pieces. I thought I knew what was the real cause and decided I would have to tell my wife what had happened in my past.

Once I did so, I had passed a point of no return. Jill had a word with a friend who put us in touch with a psychotherapist. I had tried several bouts of psychotherapy in the past, but it was the threat of the family disintegrating that made us feel we must pull together.

I can talk about it now. My psychotherapist is good. She has an excellent balance of being able to care without getting involved, and is able to steer me gently towards things. I've written quite a bit and want to write a book about my experiences. I'm not fully recovered yet though. I feel I don't have the energy I used to have. It's undermining my wife's health too. She thinks I'm going to be fully cured but I'm not sure you ever can be. The best you can hope for is to learn to live with what you are. You are different.

The worst part is not being able to respect yourself - hating yourself. If I could stop that...

Sometimes it's as though there's a quantum shift in the universe. Everything seems different. You feel as though your body's changed and you're going to die. People call it 'only a panic attack', but it was panic attacks which drove me into pubs, and from there to worse things. One night, bank, I just flung myself into the canal. I've done a lot of things like that.

When you talk about someone being a survivor, I suppose it depends on the person, but I think it's better not to do so. I've lived every day either with the fear of death, or courting it in a sense.

Recently, I've started to look to the East. They have major problems they also have far more wisdom than here. My old philosophy tutor gave me a reference infrastructure from which to make sense of life. To me life was like one vast uncharted sea. He showed me that the everyday practical is almost a mythical thing. It represents a reality, not the reality. My 'spiritual journeyings' in Eastern philosophy are building on that. I feel I need to break my attachment to quite a lot of things. I need to be able to become detached from myself.

One of the things that frightened me not so long ago was that I couldn't get a coherent picture of life. I had no coherent memories. It's like being disabled but people can't see this and have no understanding of it. If you feel 'queer' and self-loathing, you can't function properly. I can't think of any person I haven't felt inferior to. That's a very disabling condition. I have never felt I was anywhere as of right. I know I have the right now, but the feeling that I belong still isn't there. Sometimes I have nightmares, and wake up crying.

I'm ten years older than my wife. There's been some role reversal. When I was in the full flood of confidence I was a father figure I think, though she may not agree. Now I'm dependent on her. I used to go to the gym but at present I can't stand it. I can't go swimming either. I don't drive because I have panic attacks. I can't survive in the city because of the crowds. Yet I've done things like bungee jumping and diving in the past.

I realise now I've always had to run like hell to approximate standing still. I've never been very secure as

40

a macho man. You try to hide your true self and your vulnerability. I didn't have the courage then to show what I am.

I don't know whether I was actually homosexual or only so as a result of the things that had happened to me. I'd always fought shy of gay people because of the fear that my own cover would be blown. I pretended to myself that things hadn't happened that had. I've always lived my life in abject fear - that I would be totally ostracised, without support and friendship. That would have been it.

When I was at boarding school there were people who fed off the pain in others. As an adult I found such people also. There will always be the like of paedophile rings. It's part of life.

When I write my book, I want to try to communicate this. People still do not spot kids who are being abused. One of the worst things of all was that I found out that my own daughter had been abused as a child, by someone who was a lecturer in a college I was attending at the time. We never even thought it might be happening. We knew something was wrong, but assumed it was because I was under stress at the time and had shouted at her a good deal. I was totally determined nothing would happen to our kids. They were sacred. We didn't learn about it until my daughter folded under the stress and had to have psychotherapy, and it came out. I thought, 'My God, I never spotted it! I never even spotted it!'

People who abuse can be communicated with. There are some who are irredeemable in this life, but not all. There would be no way you could communicate with that one guy at boarding school; it would feed him pleasure to know someone was in pain. You could not reach my father either. If you began to get anywhere near the periphery of his being, he would reject you totally. 'I'm not talking any more,' he would say. Any hint of criticism is a total anathema to such a person, but I still think there are people you can communicate with if you try.

Can a book like this one say to someone, 'Look, you're not filth. You can get up out of the gutter and do things'? That's what's needed. I can say it to you now, but I still don't really feel it yet. Still, I can at least acknowledge a lot about myself I've never acknowledged before.

Little Girl Lost

Tessa is one of five children, and has had two daughters and three sons herself. She has a warm, generous manner and is clearly close to her own children, despite the traumatic experiences of her childhood.

As her father and first husband were both members of the RAF, Tessa has 'lived all over the place', ultimately returning to Yorkshire to settle. She can talk frankly about her memories of physical and sexual abuse by her father, but it has taken her a long time to learn to do so. She still suffers from occasional bouts of depression, though after attending group therapy, and with the support of her brother, she is learning to cope with these. After twenty-three years of confusion and self-doubt, she can at last say she is learning to like herself.

My father started hitting me first.

When I was two years old my parents separated. With my mother and brothers I went to live with my grandma for five years. Then my parents got back together and we went to Aden - my father was in the Air Force. Everything started very gradually from there. First my father was nice as a parent, then he began hitting me, and from there he went on to exposing himself.

It began with drying me after a shower, then helping me to dress but touching me when he wasn't supposed to. He would get aroused but I didn't understand that. In Aden it's really hot and when Dad had a shower he would wear a towel and walk across me as I lay on the floor. He was exposing himself - not a pretty sight.

Not having a dad until I was eight years old I didn't know how dads behaved. When your father towels you

43

dry after a bath and takes a long time, you have nothing to compare it with. For a long time I didn't realise he was doing wrong. Gradually I became afraid. I was afraid to tell my mother - she was a very self-centred person. In the five years' separation when Gran looked after us, Mum was a very vague figure. She worked all day and went out at night. She didn't have much to do with her children. When she and Dad got back together they were starting again, but with three children. A 'them and us' situation developed. Us three children stuck together. We were very very close, me and my brothers.

A few years after Mum and Dad got back together Mum had another boy. Tony was spoilt rotten. We were in Singapore at the time and Mum had a maid. At weekends we looked after the baby. She still wasn't a mother.

I used to have nightmares and went into bed with my parents. My father would put me on his side of the bed and touch me again. It was mainly touching until I was nine. Mum started visiting Grandma after that. Then Dad wanted me to sleep with him. He started trying to have sex with me but he never succeeded. I had that condition when the muscles tighten. That saved my bacon, thanks to my subconscious.

When I was thirteen my father got me pinned against a wall and ripped me. I screamed and ran and locked myself in the bathroom. Mum came. I told her I had stomach cramp and my period had started. She never suspected.

Though he never succeeded in having sex with me, my father used to make me touch him. It was absolutely gross and has an effect on me even now. I have difficulty touching a man unless he invites me. That's one hurdle I still have to cross. All the time Mum was in hospital Dad carried on trying to kiss me, which was gross too.

By the time I was fifteen, my mother was pregnant again and bleeding. She took to her bed. I had just started work at a hairdresser's and had to leave to look after the whole family. At the end of it all, the baby died. She was just two pounds full term. I was heartbroken. That baby was my only sister and I never saw her. I felt I was a part of her since I had nursed my mother. I never had the chance to say goodbye and grieve. I was sent back to work when I was no longer required.

Then Mum was pregnant again. My brother Ian was born when I was sixteen. Tony was pushed well out. But for me and my brothers, I don't know how he would have survived.

I started going out with my first boyfriend, Rob, at the age of fifteen. Dad didn't like him. He said he was a local yokel. We finished after a few weeks and then Rob was a wonderful lad to Dad. As soon as I started going out with Rob again, he was back to being an uncouth local. My father was jealous.

The last time my father hit me was when I was sixteen. It was all about a pair of pants I had left on my bedroom floor. I was supposed to take my pants off and wash them and put them on the line. (My father was watching of course.)

Dad put me over his knee and spanked me, and afterwards made me look in the mirror to see how red it was. I told my boyfriend. Rob was six foot two. He said I was to tell him if it ever happened again and he would hit my father. I told Dad what Rob had promised and he never touched me again, though I still got all the verbal abuse.

Rob wanted me to get engaged to him. He was a large chap. When he was aroused I was terrified. If he had wanted to have sex I would have run a mile, but he was such a kind and gentle person, if I had told him he would have been patient and would have helped me over it. I was so terrified of sex though, I finished with him. Perhaps if I had stayed with him I would have been with him now.

I chose my first husband when I was seventeen, because he was so quiet. I was desperate to get away from home. Simon decided that if I was expecting a child we would have to get married. It took three months of trying before I could have sex with him. When it finally happened I wasn't impressed. 'Is that it?' I thought.

All the same, I still went ahead and got married. Simon was very weak, under his mother's thumb, and I didn't even get away, as my parents insisted I stay at home with them. Then Dad talked my husband into joining up when our baby was only three months old. It changed him completely. He came back from camp a different person.

I stayed with Simon for years, having four children and living in Air Force houses while he was posted around England, and over to Germany and Ireland. I was still very withdrawn and shy. Simon was very bad with money and he went out nearly every night, leaving me alone with the children. I wanted to leave him but Mum told me it was my duty to stay with my husband. In any case, I would have to return to my parents. I ended up having a breakdown, but I still stuck it out another year.

Then I woke up one morning and looked at my husband and thought 'Yuk!' There was no communication, no affection between us. Even so it took a friend to make me go, to push me into doing so.

I came back to Yorkshire and lived with an uncle for two months, and at Mum's for one month. By that time I had met my second husband, the father of my youngest. He seemed very exciting and interesting, completely different. That didn't work either. It was a very stormy relationship. He was a real bigot, a real misanthropic Yorkshireman. Everything was my fault. At that time I was very good at guilt trips. If there was a tornado in the street I'd blame myself. I argued with him and he didn't like that, plus I was still suffering from depression after my breakdown. Jack couldn't cope with that and went off. After we had been married less than two years we split up and then had ten months together, followed by another split for three years.

Jack can be really nice but he can only stay faithful for six months. He wanted me but also wanted his bits on the side. He turns up sometimes even now, and he's asked me to go back to what was before, even though he is living with someone else. I'm not having an affair with my own husband! I told him to forget it.

I went off the rails a bit when we split up - well, a lot - drinking and having affairs. No one else was going to use me. 'If I want a man I am going to choose!' I thought.

I've learnt at therapy since that a lot of women go through this. At the time I felt I was being free. Then I cut it down because I felt the children were suffering with me being out so much. All this time my second husband kept coming back and taking off.

Finally my daughter Nicola took an overdose because of trouble at school. She was in hospital for three days. I was going through one of my own bad periods. One day I was sitting watching the video and trying not to cry. The hospital social worker came to see Nicky and I ended up bursting into tears. The social worker said, 'You need professional help. You can't go on like this.' She put me in touch with a counselling service at the local hospital. From that I moved on to psychotherapy and then to a group.

That was the beginning of my cure. Group therapy was very traumatic but it taught me a lot. The main thing it did was stop me from being ashamed. There's nothing to be ashamed of. What had happened had been done to me. I didn't ask for it. My father's the bad person, not me. That was a major step.

The person who has helped me most is my brother.

Carl's a year older than me and like me he has lived all over the place. Recently he had a heart attack, followed by a double by-pass op. It made him think. One day he told me he was being abused by our father also. It had only happened twice, once when he was an adult. He'd never told anyone before and was very upset when he told me. It did him good to talk about it. He told me Dad had also tried it with another of our brothers but Phil had got out of the car and threatened to walk all the way home if Dad touched him again.

Carl said that I shouldn't base decisions on past experiences, and that was what I had been doing. It was very simple advice, but it changed everything. I've been married twice, both times disastrously, the second one in particular. I've been seeing someone else for three years now but I don't want him to live with me because of my last husband. Now I can see this person is completely different, the same sort of character as my first boyfriend. He gets on well with my children and treats them as people. One of my last fears has gone out of the window.

I had a phobia about fire. I was terrified of fire of any sort. It used to take me a long time to light the gas cooker. I was also afraid of heights. Now my fears have gone, just evaporated. I don't get panic attacks when I'm talking to people. I'm much happier.

It's a long process that's been going on for three and a half years. I'm discovering all sorts of things about myself, and accepting them. I can accept praise from people. In the past I felt they didn't really mean it, that they just wanted something. I'm actually getting to like myself. It's taken a long, long time. When you've been told for years that you're useless you begin to believe it. I was told that by my father for more than nine years. He even took my first husband into the shed and told him what an awful person I was and that he shouldn't be marrying me.

Writing has helped me too. As a child reading books was very important to me. I was only happy in books, getting away from reality. I wanted to be those characters, not in my own life. When I was still married to my second husband I did 'O' Level English and used to love writing essays. More recently I've been to a creative writing group and started writing poems. They help me express my feelings.

A Good Girl

A little girl lost.
Alone in a wilderness.
She's reaching out,
Pleading,
Hoping someone will notice.
Needing someone to look inside her
And see all the hurt,
Twirling around,
Twisting and turning,
Making her miserable,
Making her sad.
But it's so hard to talk.
Hard to put into words
Feelings that she doesn't understand.
The fear and the shame
Is mixed up with relief,
Because it's ended.
The badness is over.
He can't hurt her anymore.
She's protected,
And loved,
And cared for.
She's a good girl.

It wasn't just me and Carl my father abused.

Two and a half years ago I ran away from home, literally, from my children and my neighbours. My second husband had already gone. I couldn't say 'No' then (though I'm learning now) and I couldn't cope with all the demands being made on me. I left my eldest son, Gary, in my house, with Danny and Nicola. Gary was nearly twenty-one. The others were sixteen and fourteen. He was quite capable of taking care of them. I came here, with my youngest boy. I was going to therapy then, but I couldn't cope with the stress any more.

Mum said Gary couldn't look after them however, and took Danny and Nicky to live with her. They were there nearly six months, but they weren't happy with my parents.

Nicky came over one day, very upset. She said she didn't like it there. A little later she came again, after phoning to say she was off school. I knew at once what she wanted to tell me. Dad was going into her bedroom while she was asleep and touching her. Nicky didn't know his ways - I'd never told her - but what she was describing was what he'd started with me.

Danny was at work at the time. I phoned him up and told him to fetch his and Nicola's clothes and come straight up here. He never asked why.

My mother wanted to know what it was about. I didn't want to tell her but ultimately I did. She said Nicky was lying. I knew Nicky wasn't because she was describing just what my father had done to me at the start. I'm just thankful I got her out early enough.

My brother Tony started the same sort of thing too. He was interfering with one of my other daughters when he was babysitting for me. Penny was seven years old at the time. Whereas I became withdrawn, Penny was very extrovert - hyperactive in fact. I never found out until I went to therapy myself. I was talking to Penny about the therapy sessions and she just sat and cried and told me. I was devastated. Until then I was best friends with Tony. He's never seen me since. That was three years ago. He must have known why Penny started going to therapy. Tony was fourteen years old at the time it happened and experimenting perhaps. It stopped when he got a girl friend soon afterwards. I'm not condoning it. What he did was totally wrong but it was different to what my father did.

Tony denies that Dad abused him, but I do wonder.

Why did my father do it?

Maybe it was because of his own childhood. I don't know. My grandmother Wilding was a very harsh woman. From things my father has told us about his own youth she was very cruel. She would scrub his neck with Vim and a scrubbing brush. He was regularly beaten. Grandmother would only sleep with Grandfather until she got pregnant. Only when she wanted another baby would she let him near. That's a long time between! Father joined the Air Force to get away when he was seventeen. He abused my aunty Susan, his sister, when he was eighteen and she was only nine years old.

A few weeks ago I wrote a long letter to my mother and sent it by hand through my brother. In it, I described everything that had happened. Mum came up to see me and said she hadn't read the letter. She'd put it away unopened because she knew it would upset her. She didn't destroy it though. I feel she knew what was in my letter, or why would it upset her?

My mother has ostrich syndrome. If she doesn't like something it doesn't exist. She'll admit to that now. Recently she was on about how she used to play with us. I can't remember one single time when she came out to play with us. We were thrown out even in the snow when Dad wanted to go to bed with her.

My father often had affairs but Mum denies all knowledge of them. She knows but won't admit she knows. She's very shallow and puts on airs and graces to which she's not entitled. Her house is like a midden sometimes but she'll complain if a spoon is dirty in a restaurant. She has a dead posh voice which she puts on for people. When we were abroad she treated the local people as if they were dirt and didn't like us talking to the maid in Singapore as an equal, yet she was a lovely person.

Mum was born in the wrong time. She has very old-fashioned ideas. I don't know how she got like that. Her own mother was the loveliest person you could meet.

I've come now to the stage when I can tolerate my father's presence for my mum's sake. I'm not afraid of him. I don't hate him. He's not worth the effort. I call him my dad but he's lost the right to be my father. I tolerate his presence because I want to have contact with my mum. It's a sense of family I think, because I don't have any other family. I've never met my cousins on my father's side. We don't know where his brothers and sisters are living.

I also don't want to lose my older brothers. I'm still very close to them. I have a very happy picture of us together when we were living with Grandma. She died when I was eleven and I still miss her, though she keeps an eye on me even now. I wish when our parents got together again that they'd left us with my Grandma. We'd have been much happier. Perhaps the reason why I get on with my mum now is that she looks so like Grandma.

I'll never forgive my father for what he did to my personality. He tried to destroy it. He never managed it though. Once I tipped out two bottles of pills and looked at them and then put them back. If you take your own life you're out of it. It doesn't hurt you, but those you leave behind. I couldn't do that to my children. I love them too much. Bringing up my own children I've over-compensated perhaps by being a bit too soft. I've got their respect however, even if I still have shouting matches with my youngest. That comes with the job when you have a fourteen year old.

When I was growing up you never heard anything about abuse. It was so shocking you never knew any

52

other girl who was abused. When I first heard about boys being abused too, I was amazed. Esther Rantzen brought it all back up for me - she brought it to the surface. In a way that did me good. It made me into a different person.

I feel the therapy group put everything that had gone wrong in my life down to the abuse, and that's not true. Abuse makes you who you are, but you do things after that yourself. Even psychotherapy didn't take me forward from the depression. The person who helped me most was my brother, just by talking to me.

The things that carry on can seem quite small to others but they're with you always. Dad's finger nails curled over. If I see a man with finger nails that curl over I won't go near him. It makes my flesh creep. My father used to flick bits of cigarette ash into my hair. Once he pinned me down on the floor and tried to make me take a drag on his cigarette. I went hysterical. I was terrified of having my hair on fire. Perhaps that is where my fear of fire comes from? I've never made the connection before. Cigarettes have absolutely disgusted me ever since. I hate anyone smoking.

Parents are supposed to teach their children right from wrong. They are not supposed to do wrong to them, then tell them it is alright because they are parents. How is the child expected to know the difference?

My childhood was stolen from me. I became an unhappy and withdrawn teenager. Then I was thrown into adulthood well before I was prepared for it. I never had time to grow up. I spent the next twenty -three years in total confusion, not knowing who I was, because I had never had the chance to find out. The small child was still locked inside me. I failed in all my relationships because each one was an escape from the last.

Now I have faced up to why I have been confused, I feel like a new person ready to discover who I really am, and I can set the little girl inside me free. I am alive.

The Survivors' Project

John runs a voluntary self-help support service for male victims of abuse. He originally set this up by himself, working from his own home. Now The Survivors' Project receives support from Leeds and Wakefield Health Authorities and from Barnardos.

John feels strongly that gay men do not have enough sources of support and is gay himself, but his project is for all men in the Leeds and Wakefield area who have experienced abuse in the past, or have been subjected to sexual attack recently. His project provides them with information, advice and support.

The motto of The Survivors' Project is 'Men Fighting Back Against Sexual Abuse'. Here John tells how he was himself abused sexually and emotionally while in local authority care, and how he found strength as an adult to fight back, and ultimately help others who had had similar experiences.

Though his story is outside many people's experience, he wishes to stress that what follows is all fact, and that nothing has been altered.

Since this piece was written male rape has become recognised in law.

I come from Sunderland originally. When I was born my mum and dad were divorcing. I was left in the hospital unwanted, so I was fostered right from my birth.

First an elderly couple looked after me until I was eight years old. Then the male of the couple died and I was put into local authority care. I have lived in about six different foster homes in all and have lost count of the children's homes I have been in.

While I was in a home between the ages of eight and thirteen I was sexually abused, repeatedly.

The home was a residential boarding school in Yorkshire, but it served a wide region and took kids from everywhere. It's closed now.

I was abused from the time I was ten years old, mostly by the man in charge. He was always known as 'The Main Man' or 'The Boss'. There were more staff than the one involved though, and it wasn't just me they abused but other boys in the home too. Teachers doubled as care assistants and some had been there for years and years and years.

It was a case of dog-eat-dog. We had sweet vouchers to spend at the tuck shops. Rewards could be taken away if we didn't go along with what we were told. It was all bribery and coercion so you didn't tell. As a punishment, we were tied to the radiators when they were on, or our feet were tied together to stop us running away. If we caused trouble we were given cold baths or showers.

Actually, the place wasn't that unhappy, but there was nothing real about it, nothing warm, no affection was shown unless you were actually doing some sort of sexual act. From the outside the school looked beautiful, a big old house set in lovely grounds with its own swimming pool even. People passing would have thought we had everything.

I blame my social worker for a lot of what happened. She used to come up to the home from Sunderland every three months for a case conference, and she never saw me, or asked if I was OK. She just did the assessment and went away.

Nobody ever asked if I was alright. At the end of term the residential school closed, so I spent the holidays in a children's home in Sunderland. They never asked why I had bruises on my body.

I used to be very ashamed of those bruises and covered them up, but I still wanted someone to ask about them. I would have told it all if someone had asked me, so long as I didn't have to go back. My fear was of not being believed. When the school holidays were over and I had to return, I used to get a sickly feeling in my stomach. I'd be genuinely sick from nerves.

No proper education was offered us at the school. The teachers/care assistants wouldn't teach but used to take us for walks in the wood, or swimming. That was great. No school. But we didn't learn anything.

I still have nightmares now and relive it all: the constant fear, butterflies in my stomach during the holidays at the thought of going back. When I was at the school the fear was worse, especially at bed time. I can picture myself lying in bed in a tight ball when the lights went out, just hoping I wouldn't be disturbed. Then there was the relief that it was morning, but still the fear of taking a shower. I still recall being sick and having diarrhoea from nerves, feeling weak and faint - being choked up, not angry. I was never angry, I just felt that I was not heard, not understood.

At thirteen I left the school and was repeatedly fostered out. At first I was with very well-to-do people who didn't understand why I had behavioural problems. They thought I was mentally retarded rather than disturbed. In fact I had been educationally deprived but I wasn't retarded. They wouldn't let me go to their son's school because I would be an embarrassment to the family. They wanted me to go to a special school.

With them, I wasn't subjected to sexual abuse, but to emotional abuse. They used to send me to bed because I didn't know my tables. There were no presents for me until I could spell my name. A child of thirteen ought to be able to spell their own name I know, but I couldn't, and they didn't understand why.

I did a lot of rebelling after that until in the end I was moved to a single parent. She adopted me when I was fourteen. It worked out fine. My life settled down with her, and education followed. She's moved to Cornwall now but I still keep in touch with her.

At sixteen I left school. I left home soon afterwards and moved to Manchester. There I had a really promiscuous lifestyle on the streets. It's hard to explain, but this lifestyle was sort of like a punishment. I felt I had to punish myself for what had happened at school. I was sleeping with men for money, while in school it was for tuck vouchers. This time I was in control however. It was pure survival sex - £2.00 for a packet of cigs, 50p for a cup of tea. I would go into nightclubs and fill an empty beer can with water and then stand outside near some man, in the hope that he would take me home so that I could have a bed for the night. It was all done as survival.

I don't want you to think that because I was doing this, what had happened to me at the school hadn't hurt me in any way. It was because of what had happened that I was doing it. I didn't believe I was worth anything. I have a low opinion of myself still, even though I've settled down. I've got a partner, have had for five years now, but I still feel I'm worth nothing. I think of myself as overweight, that I'm ugly. I have no self praise. I can't believe my partner when he says he likes me how I am.

After a few years in Manchester I got living with three men who were drag queens. I realised I could put a wig and a frock on myself and earn some money miming to records. From that I developed a proper singing act in drag, performing live. Then a residency was offered me in a nightclub for three nights a week. I became well known in Manchester for my drag act. They used to bill me as 'The really loud mouthed blond bombshell'!

After a very close friend died of AIDS however I couldn't go on living in Manchester any longer. I'd known AIDS was around, and then that my friend was HIV positive, but I hadn't realised people died of it.

So I returned to Leeds to live with my mother. By this time she had become a born-again Christian. She felt death from AIDS was a punishment, and believed for two men to sleep together was committing a big sin. I couldn't stay there long.

With my drag act I went and took over a pub in Wakefield. I turned it into a cabaret fun bar, managing it for the landlady. That's when I met my partner, and we've been together ever since.

My partner and I moved back to Leeds together. At first we lived in a quiet cul-de-sac and were victimised by the neighbours because we were gay, and they couldn't understand such things. We got a transfer to another area nearer town, and we've been living in our flat for two years now. Though we've still got a lot to do on it, it's our home. I've got four dogs and visitors have to accept that. The dogs are my family, all that I'm left with as a family. They're my children. For the very first time I can invite people into my house and ask them to obey my rules, not theirs.

When I was trying to come to terms with the emotional turmoil resulting from the abuse I'd experienced, I looked for services which would help me. I wanted to meet others who would appreciate, personally, what had happened to me. Sadly I couldn't find any. I spent ten years re-integrating my life. After I'd settled down I began to think that if others could receive support at an early stage, they could achieve what I had achieved, in a shorter time and with less suffering.

So in October 1992 I approached MESMAC and Rent Boy Action in an attempt to contact others with similar experiences. While both organisations provided support services for men who were having sex with men, neither could offer support by men who had actually experienced abuse by men.

I therefore undertook a support role for those who had been abused and were in contact with Rent Boy Action. I found this restricting however in terms of the support I was able to offer. I also wasn't reaching men who were not involved in the sex industry.

In January 1993 I began to design my own support network. I contacted the founder of Survivors (Bradford) and received advice about setting up a similar self-help support service in Leeds. Though I maintained a contact service for Rent Boy Action, I began wider advertising, distributing a thousand leaflets which I produced and paid for myself.

It has been a challenging piece of work getting the project established. First I needed some funding. I got a lot of people from health and AIDS type services together in one room and discussed my idea with them. Then I challenged them to take it on board and fund me.

Wakefield and Leeds Health Authorities both gave me £500 for a seven month project, and Barnardos have provided me with a room and a desk. Wakefield Health Authority have also helped me design the Survivors' Project logo, and do the printing and further leaflets.

The result has been an increased interest in the Survivors' Project. I receive on average twenty-seven calls a week now and meet with about fifteen individuals a month. Clearly such a service as I am offering is needed.

In March my funding runs out and I have no idea whether I will be able to carry on. However, I have been asked to speak at conferences of paediatric workers, prison and probation staff and the police federation. There has been a lot of interest in what I'm trying to do. I still have difficulty spelling and writing things down, because of my disrupted education, so I use overhead projectors when I'm talking in public. That way, I can prepare things beforehand.

My present work has helped me to come to terms with what happened to me. I see people so much worse than myself. My only anger is when people are crying out for help and no one will listen. I get angry with doctors and psychiatrists who can't see that a person has got a problem, simply because he is a man. There is still a problem of macho attitudes. I've done a lot of work recently with people like the West Yorkshire Police however, who are taking it on board as an issue.

I feel frustration too with the lack of services around any sort of male sexual abuse. There is a lack of understanding and lack of equal rights. All the research into male sexual abuse when AIDS and HIV first came up is very useful, but what is needed is extra funding to do proper work. We have to learn by our instincts too: that a man might need help, and a support worker or befriender. We need to ask and see.

One of my contacts died at the beginning of the year. He was a fifteen year old rent boy. He had been in a gang rape and went to the services who deal with male sex. They said they couldn't help because he was under twenty-one. He threw himself off a train bridge. Another victim I know of was married, with a child. Because he had been abused by his own father, when his son became the same age he}d been when his own abuse started, he became scared of the child and couldn't show his feelings. Psychiatric help was denied him because no one recognised there was a problem. So he decided his son would be better off without him and killed himself.

One victim said to me, 'It's bad enough being a victim of rape, but it's worse when people don't believe it's a crime.' A victim is a victim twice - a victim of the attack and of how society judges that attack.

Male rape doesn't exist in law. Our law dates from Queen Victoria's time. Sexual assaults on men commonly take the form of buggery, that is anal penetration. The law doesn't recognise enforced buggery as a serious crime equivalent to female rape. Therefore, in law, there are no male rape victims.

Rape isn't a sexual thing however - it's a power trip. It is not often that the perpetrator gets a sexual turn-on. Preying on a victim is what turns them on. I have figures showing that forty-two per cent of the perpetrators of male sexual abuse are heterosexual. It is a big myth that all gay men abuse. Family and friends are the worst offenders; then friends of the family, then date rape. This isn't recognised at all. 'An unknown man' is right at the bottom of the list, yet this is what people fear most because it is what the press highlights.

Although the number of men sexually assaulted each year is relatively low in comparison to women, the psychological after-effects for men are devastating. Fuelled by the widespread prejudice and discrimination against gay men in society, they find it particularly difficult to report an incident of abuse or rape. This can lead to more self-blame and helps generate well-founded feelings of self-pity or defensive rage.

It is important that my clients know I am a survivor myself - a Barnardos child coming back to be based at the Barnardos St James' Project. (My later fostering and adoption was through Barnardos.) The work I am doing is totally voluntary - I don't get paid for all this. My funding is going on phone bills, photocopying paper, public transport and so on. So far the £1000 has enabled me to speak at a number of conferences and publish a report, in addition to helping individuals. Hospitals are beginning to contact me too when men come into casualty.

A thousand pounds is pennies really when you come to think of the work that has come out of it. It just shows what can be done. I would like to go on to establish a prototype service - not just a self-help project - to identify needs and how best they can be met.

Dad's Little Angel

Natasha is still struggling to overcome the after-effects of abuse by both her father and her uncle. Though she is married and has a daughter of her own, recent events in her life have brought her childhood sense of panic and insecurity back to her.

Many of Natasha's memories are vague, still too deeply suppressed for her to recall details. She is determined to come to terms with her experiences however and is attending counselling sessions to help her to do so. Though it is clearly an effort, she has begun to force herself to talk honestly and openly about what happened. When she is ready, she intends to have hypnotherapy treatment to help her fill in the gaps in her memory, though she has been warned that doing so may cause her a lot of pain.

Since she gave the interviews from which her account has been written, she and her husband have got back together, and have begun to 'sort things out'. A quietly spoken and slightly built woman, Natasha has a great deal of courage. She is determined once and for all to reclaim her past, so that she can put it behind her.

It all started with my sister. Janie was born deaf when I was five. No one knew at the time that she was deaf. They thought she was mentally retarded.

My mother couldn't cope. She was very upset and had a lot of problems with her nerves. As a result, my sister was in and out of care. She spent years in a special hospital, until she was eight or nine, when her deafness was discovered. After that, Janie was fostered.

Her foster parents would have loved to adopt her, but Mum and Dad wouldn't let them. I went to visit her often with Dad, but Mum couldn't cope with seeing her.

Sometimes Janie came home to stay with us, but she used to scratch herself - go berserk basically, so she stayed in the foster home until she was fourteen or fifteen. One time she came home for a few months to see how she would get on. It was very upsetting for me. I couldn't get on with my school work as we were sharing a room. I couldn't cope with her myself.

I'm not sure what happened after that as I have a gap in my memory there. I was about thirteen when Dad started abusing me. I don't remember much, only a few times when Mum was in hospital. I was growing up and my father was highly sexed. He needed an outlet and I was that outlet. It was never in the house, only outside. I think my mother knew but didn't want to know.

I just can't understand how I cared so much for Dad. Part of me feels he can't really have done all the bad things he did. He seemed brilliant to me in other ways. He put me on a pedestal. I was his little angel and he used to carry photos of me around with him. I wasn't Mummy's little girl, I was Daddy's. I could talk to Dad, but not to my mother.

It wasn't just Dad though. My uncle had a go too. I tried to tell my aunty but she didn't want to know - basically no one wanted to know. With my uncle it happened just occasionally. He used to pick me up from school and I think it happened then. Again there are just blanks in my memory. I can't remember much.

I left school at fifteen. I couldn't take any exams because I suffered panic attacks. Every time I tried to take an exam my head started going round and round. In myself I decided I was totally useless and gave up.

After leaving school I tried to do typing at college, but once again I had to give it up. I had a few jobs, but nothing worked out, though when I was fifteen and a half I worked for my dad on a market stall and enjoyed that. Mum was getting poorly again, having a lot of problems with her nerves.

When I was eighteen I got engaged. Everyone in the Social Club was doing it, so I did it too. My fiance was a student and quite poor. Dad bought the engagement ring for us. I wasn't in love. Dave found out he was bisexual and had a nervous breakdown. For three months he stayed with us at our house. Then I decided he was not the one for me and left him.

Dad died when I was twenty, while he and Mum were abroad. They were on a second honeymoon and he drowned. When I heard he was dead, my uncle said I should fly out there to him. In fact, when I arrived my father was still alive, on life support in hospital. I ran out of the ward when I saw him. I couldn't bear to see him with all the tubes and had another panic attack. Mum was very upset too, but the assistant manager at the hotel took me under his wing, and helped me a lot.

I took Dad's death really hard and didn't want to go out for months. Mum said I must, but I felt like my life had gone too - that I loved him and missed him terribly. I don't understand why my father's death upset me so much when he was abusing me, but it did.

I tried then to talk to Mum about what had happened with Dad. She wouldn't listen. She said it was a load of rubbish and didn't want to know, so I gave up and didn't try to tell her any more.

Mum was suffering from breast cancer and it got worse when Dad died. After a few months she started to go out quite a bit and enjoy herself. She used to go out with me sometimes. She didn't look old at all. Then she met my stepfather.

Mum's new man didn't want to know me. He was attracted to Mum because she had her own car and house. She knew she only had a few months to live so she got married to him quickly. When Mum died, my stepfather got the house and everything.

The whole business has turned me into something I don't know if I really like. It's left me with panic attacks and agoraphobia, and affected my marriage, sexwise particularly. I can't believe anyone really likes me, and I'm trying to work this out even now.

When I first married I still suffered panic attacks and agoraphobia, but I managed to overcome them. I've been having a reasonable life the last few years, but recently things have suddenly got a lot worse, and the agoraphobia has come back. Everything has just happened at once.

My marriage is breaking up you see. I've decided that's it though we're staying together. We'll be leading separate lives, doing what each one of us wants to do though acting like everything's OK for Susie's sake. We were thinking of getting a divorce but my husband wouldn't have anywhere to stay - he'd have no money. I'm the one doing this. I've fallen in love. It's totally ridiculous and stupid as it's never happened to me before.

I married my husband because I cared for him. That's different to love. Our marriage had been breaking up for a while but the main breaking point for me was when I stayed with Paul for one night. That was when I realised my relationship with my husband was over. I was very happy when I was with Paul, though I couldn't see him as often as I wished.

We've broken up now however. For the first week after the break I was suicidal. I cried for days.

My husband knows all about Paul. In a way it's good that things have come to a crisis. I needed to tell him that things were not working. Now he wants to change, though for himself I think, not for me. He doesn't want to stay but he knows he has to, because he can't do anything else.

Falling in love with Paul has made me think more about myself. I've been trying to figure out whether I loved my parents, or just cared for them, and what I feel for Paul. I just know that it is definitely love and that I haven't felt this way before. It happened very quickly. within a matter of three weeks. We hit it off so well together. I could talk to Paul and I couldn't talk to other people.

That's why I'm going to counselling. I'm trying to come to terms with all that's happened. It's helping to talk things through, to find out certain things. There's quite a bit of sorting out to do still though. I need a lot of sessions, and the extra counselling I'm planning to go to can cost anything between five and fifteen pounds a session. That's a lot when you're only earning about thirty pounds a week of your own. I'd like to go long term too, for quite a while - a couple of years perhaps, so it's going to mount up.

Fortunately I've found a place recently that will let me pay a cheap rate, based on what I can afford. My first visit there was brilliant. I'd hoped to speak to a woman, but the man I saw was very understanding and helpful and I told him so many things. He won't actually be my counsellor, but I think I may be better speaking to a man rather than a woman in future, though that surprises me. They're setting up long-term counselling for me.

I'm also interested in hypnotherapy to fill in the gaps in my memory. I've been warned it may hurt, but I'm willing to face the pain of memory. It's what I want. I'm finding that's even more expensive though, and I can't afford it at the moment. The private clinics charge thirty pounds an hour. The local hospital doesn't do hypnotherapy, though it offers psychotherapy, but there's a waiting list of three months. The long-term counselling service I have just started doesn't offer hypnotherapy either, but they say they will be able to relax me and that may help me to remember.

I arranged to see my doctor and examine my medical records in the hope that they might tell me something about my childhood, but I didn't learn a lot. The visit was very hurried. I was only allowed ten minutes and there were masses of records. All I could do was look through one section, the early 1970s. They were absolutely awful years for my mother. She was terribly depressed it seems, and taking loads of tablets. Basically, Mum couldn't cope, full stop. When my sister was born everything stopped for her. I'm sure her cancer and death followed on from that. I felt sick for a week after I had read the records, but I didn't really get any further about myself.

It was very strange reading the doctors' opinions about me. At the age of thirteen I was manipulating my mother. As soon as there was anything wrong I was taken to the doctor. She must have been seeking attention. There were suggestions in the records that I hated my mum, and blamed her for my father's death (which I'm sure I didn't), and statements like, 'Natasha can't cope with her mother.' I kept thinking 'This isn't me.' Nowadays I feel I'm basically quite nice, like most people. I can't think I would manipulate people.

Still, I'm glad I went and I would like to see more another time. I'd love to take the whole folder back home if possible, but I don't suppose that's allowed. Ten minutes is far too short a time to do more than have a quick glance through.

No one can understand it all except me, and even I can't. I'm learning however that other people did things when they were younger, and they weren't considered wrong, while I was. Women in their twenties do things now I wasn't allowed to do, like reading *Cosmopolitan*. Mum told the doctor I was rebelling - in my twenties! Girls rebel at sixteen today, or even younger. I'm sure all I was trying to do was assert myself. All I wanted was to be happy.

I still don't know what I feel towards my parents. I threw everything to do with them away, the glass cabinet, pictures, everything, so they couldn't trigger memories. I don't know if I hate or love them. They were my parents, that's all. I've avoided getting in touch with old friends as they knew my family and must know some of what happened, but I will have to face up to it, and meet them one day. If only my aunty would tell me a bit more, but she won't. Mum was her sister after all.

My vision for the future is to be a normal, healthy person, to feel OK, to cope. I want to make decisions for myself instead of always apologising if things go wrong. I've always said 'please' and 'thank you' like a scared little rabbit. This is something I've got to work on, and I'm beginning to do it, to have confidence to do things for myself, without asking first. I've been in one job now longer than in my whole life.

I even invited myself down to London to see Paul. It was the first time I'd had the courage to go away on my own. I was in a state of shock for three days afterwards! I felt very pleased with myself, and that's very unusual. I couldn't believe I hadn't had a panic attack, even with the journey all that way on my own. I had a really good weekend - the best weekend we've ever had - though poor Lewis was very upset about it. I know I've got the confidence to travel on my own again.

I'll get there! I'm doing things I've never ever done before. Though I still get panic attacks sometimes and I'm very unhappy without Paul, I'm getting more confident all the time.

After Paul and I broke up I felt the only way to get over it was to work and fill my days, so I contacted an agency. They got a job for me straight away. Now I'm cleaning two full days as well as in the evenings. That's made me feel a lot better. Lewis has helped me a lot too.

Because I had missed a few times, the Crisis Centre I had been going to set me up with someone else, but by the time I got a session with them, the crisis was over and they said I was coping. The relationship with Paul has at least taught me that I can feel love, and that's something.

Lewis and I may after all separate, he's getting so fed up, and we may divorce later. I phoned up a solicitor's and they said we could live together even after we were divorced, but that it might cause problems over the ownership of the house. I wanted to know in case it would help Lewis. There's no way I'll ever get married again. It's just not worth it, not unless some miracle happens.

Maybe in the future I'll try to study something again, though at the moment I can't concentrate very much. I've thought of joining the Samaritans, but I feel that I need to be more completely recovered before I do. I'm also interested in going into counselling myself some day. I think I would have an understanding of other people. Nowadays I get on really well with people - though I didn't while I was living at home. I was very introverted then, and only started coming out of myself when I left. When I can, I may explore the idea of counselling more.

Really, I'd just like to be OK, that's all, for my daughter's sake. I want her to grow up with no hassle. Sometimes I think that after twenty years I should be over it all, but what happened in my childhood has affected my whole life. That's why I'm so determined to get it sorted out now.

Playing Happy Families

Alan has achieved a great deal professionally. After completing his university studies, he was employed at the Government's Radio and Space Research Station, Slough. There, he established and organised the Satellite Prediction Service, which became the UK and international centre for space research into atmospheric and geodetic analysis. From Slough Alan moved to the London Planetarium, becoming a consultant to TV news and current affairs programmes when space launches were taking place. He has also worked for the Radio Corporation of America at the Fylingdales Satellite Station, North Yorkshire. Following this appointment, Alan designed and established the Scarborough Planetarium, directing this for seven years.

Throughout all these appointments, Alan served as consultant to the Ministry of Defence Royal Aircraft Establishment. He was employed by the now defunct Space Department as author and researcher of the Table of Artificial Earth Satellites, and the Table of Space Vehicles, and has written many articles in scientific journals and the popular press.

Yet throughout his life, Alan has had to cope with the effects of the emotional abuse he suffered in his childhood, and the continued strain caused by his relationship with his mother. Now in his fifties and semi-retired, he is still finding it difficult to come to terms with the painful memories her death has recalled.

My mother was called Mary Evelyn. She was born in 1905 and came supposedly from a well-to-do background. Her father was a shop owner. That was much more privileged than today. They had a home furnishing shop in a prominent position in Marsden, near Huddersfield. My mother's mother was a seamstress, who did lovely embroidery. There was only one other child, George.

My mother grew up during the mid twenties and even went to Leeds University. Only three per cent of the population went in those days and it was much less for women. She took a BSc in Botany, followed by a Teacher's Diploma. All that time her own mother was unwell, coming and going. It wasn't allowed to interfere with my mother's prospects. The looking after was done by her brother.

Then my mother met my father, Jack. Legend has it that it was on a train. When we cleared out the house after her death we found a great deal of archive stuff, including typical romping on the beach photos. They looked like the conventional happy twenties couple then. In 1933 they married. My father came from a more working class background and Mother always considered she had married beneath herself.

My mother lost one of her parents - I think it was her mother - the year before she and Dad married. Her father died the year after. Within a handful of years, she had a miscarriage and lost a boy. She talked about this on occasion when I was a child. She used to accuse my father of everything that went wrong. It was always his fault if the world was not right. I gather she thought he had been to blame for her losing the baby, because he took her upstairs on a double decker bus and it swung about.

In September 1938 I was born, at Littleborough near Rochdale. My mother went back to teaching in a well-to-do private girls' school after I was born.

Within a year, war had broken out. My father was called up soon and went away to the Middle East. I can remember as a little lad of three or four years old running up and down corridors of girls' schools and having the time of my life. I was farmed out with anyone who would have me. Sometimes I was looked after by a nanny I called 'Aunty Alice' - I was quite fond of her.

One of the things I came across in the house was a letter from my mother to Dad while he was in service as a quarter master in Iraq. It was quite amazing - a blistering letter on the lines of, 'You'll have to write to the War Office and get them to cancel the war as it's very inconvenient to me. Your little lad wants a brother. He's pestering me all the time for one. Don't take no for an answer. This is an emergency!' She said it about fifty-three times in ten pages, with underlinings. It was a classic - as though poor Dad could do anything about it.

That was in 1943 when I was only five. Nothing happened. Father couldn't do much by post and Monty wouldn't let him come home!

We'd moved to another house when I was about seven or eight years old, further into Rochdale. My father was almost due to come back from the war by then. Round about this time, I was given a kitten by a neighbour. A kitten was better than a brother! But my mother wouldn't have it. The kitten had to go back. I was so disappointed. All my life I was never allowed to have pets. I managed to have a frog in a tin once, but it escaped overnight. To some extent I was a latchkey kid, and I was missing having company.

I had friends at school of course, but my mother's house was total chaos and I couldn't bring them home. There was no chair to sit on and the table was always covered in assorted gunge. There was no place to have a proper meal or to do any work. It was her thing to say, 'You can't have friends to play here. You must go over to their place.' 'It isn't convenient,' was her favourite phrase.

So if I had friends I had to go to them or play in the garden. That doesn't enable a child to develop relationships in the normal course of events.

Then my father came back from the war, in about 1945. All hell broke loose. When he was abroad my mother could only write him blistering letters, but when he was home it was like match and tinderbox. They used to rub each other up the wrong way.

My father had done night classes in his youth in accountancy, and he became a company secretary in a weaving shed of a firm making heavy brocade cloth. It would have been quieter for Dad if he'd stayed away. My mother wasn't in the least domesticated. She didn't have the basics in cooking, looking after a kid. She used to say, 'Cooking is a bit beneath me. People of my category have servants to do that sort of thing.' We used to go out to the chip shop or get a couple of muffins to eat. The place went to a shambles.

My parents were always rowing about one thing or another. There were no formal meals. It was every man for himself. I got whatever I could to eat. My classic memory is of tinned Heinz sponge pudding. I survived on those. They were happily scattered all over the house and I used to eat them cold and uncooked. My father survived by having his lunch at the mill in the canteen. At least he got one cooked meal a day.

My mother was no great seamstress either, despite her own mother's abilities. I remember growing bigger and never having a new shirt, just adding a piece of elastic to make the buttons meet.

Then there was the case of the dreaded dentist. When I was eleven or so I had to go for some treatment. I had to go by myself. I had gas, yet it was up to me to get there and back by myself. I can remember sitting in a bus shelter until I recovered a bit. It was one more example of 'every man for himself'.

My mother seemed to love mice. I suppose that was why I couldn't have a kitten. It got worse over the years from the time I was eight to eighteen. The house just got untidier and untidier until mice moved in. She loved those little mice. When my father was unhappy he used to go to bed early. My mother would stay up until two or three o'clock in the morning. Her favourite thing was to watch the little mice playing. It ran through her life - a creeping thing that grew.

We moved from Rochdale to Bolton. By the the the age of eighteen I had lived in five different houses. We were 'always flitting' as they used to say. My mother used to say moving house was the only chance to clear out her drawers, but she never did clear out. The removal men used to have apoplexy and just dump a pile of packing cases for everything to go in. The rubbish went from house to house without getting any less.

With each new house, my mother would advertise in the local paper: Cleaning lady wanted for 'light' domestic work, two hours a week. It was just a game of class superiority. The poor Mrs Mop could do nothing more than spin helplessly in circles, while Mother breathed down her neck.

When I was clearing out after my mother's death a friend suggested that my parents' flitting was because they were not happy in the house - it was a nest building procedure. They hoped that by moving they would make a happy house in the new place. I'm not sure who initiated the moves. My father liked the wheeling and dealing of negotiating. It was probably six of one and half a dozen of the other.

The rows between them got worse and worse. They used to chase each other round and round the house squealing and bawling. I was the little piggy caught in the middle. At times they weren't speaking to each other and it would be, 'You tell your mother this,' and 'You tell your father this.' They used to leave notes for each other all over the house.

Generally I got on fairly well with my father. I admired him professionally but I couldn't get close to him because of the circumstances. My father wanted to be liked by others. He was admired at the mill. He used to say to me, 'When you grow up, lad, don't you get married.'

By that time I had passed my Eleven Plus, and between 1952 and 1957 I went to Bolton School. It was fee paying but I had won a scholarship. The school was well respected - Ian McKellan was in my class. I couldn't bring anyone home though. It was never 'convenient'. If I did, I got the door slammed in my face with 'I'm busy!'

I was fond of my grandfather on my dad's side. He was called Walter and I have happy memories of him making lovely rice puddings in a smoky old range. Grandma was blind, and had been pretty well all my childhood. Grandfather died though when I was nine so I grew up through adolescence on my own. I had to socially educate myself however I could.

When I was twelve I started trying to do things for myself. I was interested in films and astronomy and used to make up scrapbooks. If I got the wrong side of my mother there was trouble though. Once she took a dislike to one of the pictures in my scrapbook and tore it out before my eyes. I can't remember the reason but she threw a scrapbook I was working on out of the upstairs open window onto the concrete outside. The book burst at the seams and everything was ruined. Five years of my work was just belted through the window. It wasn't the money I'd spent on it that mattered most. Seeing my work totally ruined led me to put two and two together: 'What I've done means bugger all to her.'

I was never sexually abused, but what she was doing damaged me. It was a domineering psychological thing. If I didn't do instantly what my mother wanted she would say, 'Wait till your dad gets home and you'll get the belt.' One day she had made that threat and when my father came home she told him to thwack me. Dad tried to look serious and sent me to my bedroom. My mother hadn't got the moral courage to belt me herself.

When my father came upstairs he said, 'Your mother says you've got to have ten of the best. Bend over the bed.' He'd decided he wasn't going to do it though and thwacked the bed. 'I suggest you make appropriate noises,' he commented. So I squealed, and then he went downstairs. My mother's honour was saved and Dad thought it was all a storm in a teacup. He was into the business of self-preservation from his own point of view - anything for a peaceful life.

I had to make my own teenageness. I used to get some pocket money of course, but if things got desperate I used to visit Freddie Fox's local pawnshop and second-hand emporium, and cash in some of my unwanted toys or scrapbooks. I thought at the time he was giving me a shilling or halfcrown more out of sympathy than good business. Later I did jobs in the school holidays - humping bales of cotton in a mill, or sacks of flour in a bakery, or doing the Christmas post.

I used to love the cinema, and taught myself to navigate from town to town. There were fifty cinemas in the Manchester area in those days. Every night there was a different film showing somewhere. There was a favourite transport cafe where I used to get egg and chips afterwards.

I used to train spot too and collect bus numbers and so on. I joined youth clubs at churches and got involved in a skiffle group - I sort of grew up there. The only way I could learn about relationships was from the cinema and youth clubs. I still couldn't have people home or ask my mother about problems. If I did ask her about people she used to give me a distorted view of them. I found I had to unlearn such views later.

When it was time for me to leave school I decided I wanted to do Astronomy at university, and in September 1957 I started at Edinburgh. My parents gave me no financial support - nothing regular. I applied for a grant from the Local Council which paid for my fees and term time, and in the holidays I had to get various jobs to fill in.

When I was leaving for university my mother had a great suspicion of me, and thought I might 'disappear things' from the house. Having managed to get digs in Edinburgh, I packed my own suitcase and said I was leaving home, that I couldn't stick the house any longer. My mother asked, 'Have you got anything of mine in that suitcase?' Finally she called the police. I just sat on the front doorstep and when the policeman turned up I explained to him and got him to go through my suitcase and verify that everything inside was mine. Then I left.

I used to come back at the end of term, and my landlady would keep my room on hold in return for a retainer. One term just before Christmas I came home all the way from Edinburgh to Bolton. Within twenty-four hours I had had enough and walked out again. I had no money in my pocket after paying the rail fare. So I hitchhiked back to Edinburgh and my landlady.

There was a girl in Bolton I'd met and liked. She was going up to Edinburgh for a job and we kept in touch there. We got on alright, but it fell through as these things do. By then I was in my second year at college. I went on a space conference in Amsterdam and met another girl on the plane. We started writing to each other afterwards and then meeting.

By then I was nearly twenty-one years old. I decided I ought to take Jill home to meet my parents. I took her to the house in Bolton and knocked on the door. And what did my mother do? She slammed the door on us with 'It's not convenient.' I had been trying to impress my girlfriend and instead I trundled off with my tail between my legs.

My mother's curiosity got the better of her though and subsequently she did meet her. Then our two sets of parents got together. That was another excruciating thing. My mother got her parents to one side and told them all sorts of stories blackening my character. Even Jill's parents could see this was unusual and were sympathetic to me.

In 1959 I was twenty-one. It was the fashion to have Coming of Age parties at that time, a prime opportunity for Mother to assemble the rich and famous, and then bathe in their reflected glory. My mother's whole life was a charade - she put up a façade to the outside world that she was wonderfully educated and upper class. My father was in the Rotary and had good connections at the mill. We looked externally like a well to do family. So my mother hired the Co-op hall in Bolton for a twenty-first party. She called in all the big wigs and her friends. At the time I was still going out with Jill but she was always my second choice. My thoughts were on the first girl still and I was really hoping it would all fall through.

The party was a dreadful occasion. Everyone was in dicky bows and evening dress and there was a hired band. I had invited Joyce as an old friend. I really wanted to see her but Jill and her parents were there too. At a certain point my father stood up and made a welcome speech. Out of the blue he said, 'And what more suitable occasion to announce Alan's engagement?'

I practically fell through the floor boards. I could do nothing. I couldn't say 'It's a load of cobblers' in front of all the big wigs. It would have taken an enormous amount of courage to do so.

I don't know why my father did it. He was a victim himself. Because of my mother he never got close to me and therefore didn't know of Joyce. I had never told my mother for fear of her destroying everything. As a child I used to hide my toys from her after she threw my book through the window.

I didn't have the courage to undo it. I was afraid Jill would laugh at me too now. So I had to go along with it. It was all smiles on Jill's and her parents' faces. I had some quick words with Joyce, but I couldn't say much about what I really felt and she just wished me every happiness.

I did marry Jill, at the end of the term after I graduated. My marriage nearly broke up after three years but we stuck it out for eleven years. The break up was pretty acrimonious and turned into a battle between my mother and my in-laws. When I searched the house after my mother's death I found lovely vitriolic letters, a whole can of worms. My mother was one for tittle tattle and everything you said used to be distorted and passed to the Rotary Club. For instance I found Margaret, my second wife, was being referred to as 'the other woman' even though we didn't meet until after the break up.

Why did my parents stay together? In the fifties divorce was almost unknown, though I couldn't have blamed my father if he had split up from my mother. There would have been all hell let loose if he had tried to break up though. In any case, he was one of the classic old school. He had made certain vows and my mother was his wife. He must have had some remnants of feeling for his wife despite everything. Or perhaps the large satin wedding anniversary cards we found in the clearance were just an expression of an ideal relationship that could never exist.

I stuck it out as long as I was at school - I had to - but then I got out, though I could never completely leave because of Dad. If I had walked out of my twentyfirst party I would have been slamming the door on my father and I didn't want to. Many times I wondered if I should let them have my forwarding address but I always did. On occasions when I had achieved something on my own by my own hard work - like my graduation - I would have liked to do it without my mother being there but it would have cut my father out. It was the same with my wedding. If I had hated both of them I could have said, "To hell with it all," but I was caught by my feelings for my father.

I found wonderful testimonials to Dad in the house. They said, "He lives for his work" in effect, and that was true. It was all he had, plus his local club. He used to play billiards there and have a drink but he never came home in a drunken rage or anything like that. He was just getting some sanity.

My father wasn't wealthy. He wasn't very well paid. (I found hundreds of old wage slips in the house so I know what he earned.) He also had to help my grandmother. He paid most of the cost of her staying in a blind people's home. Grandma lived to an enormous age, right to 1971 when she died at ninety-three. Dad only lived eight years longer than her.

Jill and I were living in Scarborough but when we broke up I moved to Leeds. My parents had had five or six more moves since I left for university at eighteen. They never did find whatever it was they were looking for. They visited me in Leeds a couple of times but I couldn't take Margaret to their house. When I suggested it, my mother would always say they would be out or that it was inconvenient. You can't travel on spec on a three hour journey by bus. That put a block on me seeing my father. The only alternative was for them to come to my house, or for us to meet on neutral ground.

Dad retired at sixty-five but he had no home to retire to and he almost begged the mill to keep him on. It was his life. Afterwards he tried to find jobs to keep him out of the house. Finally he got one with a bloke running a handyman firm. He was working until the day he died.

My father died at home. He'd had an attack in his bedroom. My mother phoned at seven am. It was the first time she had ever asked me to come, so we went over at once. We knew the address but we didn't know the way.

When we arrived and knocked on the door my mother greeted us with her usual scowl. She could have killed at a hundred yards with that face. She only asked me to do one thing for her, to go through my father's suit and jacket pockets to see what was there. Dad's employer came round. He was very upset and shocked. I remember him saying, 'Well, he didn't have any bloody life here.'

One of Dad's few joys was a stamp collection - British Commonwealth. He had lovely big albums all spaced out immaculately. He'd achieved it despite his circumstances. There wasn't a clean table in the house so he used to work on his bed sometimes. It was a valuable collection in its own right and his life's work as well, so it was doubly important to him. He had been through the collection only recently with the intention of selling. It was all valued up. My mother asked me to sell it for her. There were two huge heavy suitcases of albums and we had to lug them to the bus.

Within a day or two she was on the phone: 'I've been on to the solicitor and he says you shouldn't have taken anything out of the house. I'm talking quietly because we don't want the policeman next door to hear.'

It was just the same as when I was a kid, that hint of a threat. I knew perfectly well she was quite prepared to cut off her nose to spite her face. She had once laid out £150 in solicitor's fees rather than pay for £25 worth of damage claimed by a holiday hotel from her. So I hired a friend and his van to take the collection straight back to the house. I actually surprised her into being in when we arrived.

My mother put the albums into an auction house but she only got about a third of their value. She had enough things; she didn't have to get rid of the albums like that. She was throwing Dad's life away once again.

The funeral was a farce, more like a charabanc outing to the seaside. The procession started off from a chapel of rest in Nelson and then went to Earby Church. There was a steep flight of steps up to the church and the bearers had to carry the coffin up them and then back down. The service took longer than anticipated and we were losing time all the while. Finally we hurriedly set off for the crematorium. Mother saw someone she knew and stopped the car to natter through the window. By the time we set off again for Skipton crematorium we were ten or fifteen minutes late. The cortege was belting along to make up time and nearly rammed into a stationary tarmac van. There wasn't an ounce of dignity for poor Dad.

When my mother herself died I decided not to plant her next to Dad for her to be nagging him all eternity. I put her somewhere else so he could have a bit of peace.

A year or two after Dad's death Mother was always going off on holidays, leaving the house in a terrible state. She used to go on half a dozen a year. On a cruising holiday in the Canaries she met a bachelor about her age - seventy-fiveish - and got her clutches into him. He didn't live far away from her and they went on a few holidays together and to Scarborough on several visits. Then she wanted to bring him to me in Leeds. I didn't mind one way or the other but the day she chose I simply couldn't have her. I had a deadline to meet for work. When I explained, she insisted, 'It's already booked; the hotel and buses are all booked.' So I said, 'You can still come if you want, but I shall slam the door in your boyfriend's face.' It was some revenge after thirty years.

She used to telephone me at about eleven o'clock at night and rant on for about an hour. She'd work me up into a total frenzy until I couldn't sleep. During the last year I said I'd had enough for one lifetime and after that it was relatively quiet on the western front.

Her house was so chaotic every facility had gone to pot. There were no clean cooking facilities or bath. Neighbours would invite her for tea, or see her smartly laundered to go on holiday, or even deliver a hot meal to her door - only to have their kindness thrown back in their faces. It wasn't just us, it was everybody she treated like that. She used to invite herself round for tea and would sit and have her fill. Once that was achieved, she would tease and insult them. It was like she enjoyed sticking pins in them to see how they reacted.

My mother wouldn't let anyone into her own house however, wouldn't let the electricity or gas meters be read. She would hide when they said they were coming. They'd been trying to get in for two years. She was spending £300 a quarter on gas and £300 on electricity so I suppose she was afraid of the meters being read.

Then she died suddenly, at the age of eighty six, in a road accident. We were thrown into a bizarre house clearance. The whole of the ground floor was like a giant mouse nest. Hardly any furniture was visible but mountains of torn and scrap paper dissolved one room into another. All the internal doors were open. There were pathways where this 'giant mother mouse' had gone about her house.

At first we didn't know how or where to start, but gradually over the period of a year, with regular visits, we did bottom it. We filled 206 dustbin bags of rubbish - rubbish, not things you could save: half eaten pork pies, bits of mouldy cheese, things like that. There were no live mice by then, just one little skeleton in front of the fire trying to keep warm.

When we cleared the house we found documentation regarding neighbours who had complained about the mice. The Pest Control Department had slapped orders on her to clear up or they would fumigate the place. The council had had to do the same in each house she had lived in. At one time big burly men moved in and dumped stuff in a skip outside. My mother went off screaming down the road, and a kind neighbour had to intervene to help her. This lady told us how they had laid poison and set traps; my mother had protested at having to have the mice killed, but had realised the council would take action if she didn't.

You needed wellington boots and a peg on your nose to go into that house. It wasn't that bad when I was a child. In those days she hadn't had thirteen rooms or thirty years to collect it all in, but it was the same pattern.

We found modern stuff next door to letters from 1942. There were carbon copies of letters sent to people over the years, and scribbled drafts. Dad was very methodical and Mother had kept everything. There were even letters that had been returned to her for some reason by people they'd written to.

We're only just getting all the photos sorted and I am on many of them, like my parents' silver wedding or a cousin's wedding. There's visible proof I was there but I don't remember it. It's almost as if my mind has wiped it out. I must have gone to my parents' party. There I am with a cigarette in my hand yet if you had asked me I would have said I didn't smoke.

It's taken me two years to sort it all out, and to come to terms with it all. Getting over my mother's death hasn't been the problem, rather remembering living with someone who, shall we say, was eccentric at the very least. When you grow up in certain circumstances it affects your whole life.

You don't survive. You learn to cope. I don't know how I will feel in ten years' time. Things do get better but you can't get totally away from it.

In my experience, other people who have had strong relationships with their parents have been equally affected, like my second wife, who had a happy childhood but lost her father at sixteen. He exerted such a strong influence on her that she misses him still. The net result is the same.

My advice is to separate yourself as much as possible physically. If you live three doors down the road you are never going to win. You've got to get yourself sufficient distance away. That sounds like running away from the problem, but there is an optimum distance; you mustn't

84

be able to get there and back in a day. Part of my survival mechanism is also to have a bit of healthy cynicism. If you say, 'That person's done that awful thing to me' forever, you're not going to do any good to yourself. You must learn to shrug things off.

The other thing is that, whether abused or not, you go through life and encounter problems. I have been very lucky. When the crisis has overtaken me, someone from the shadows has emerged and been a great help, often a complete stranger - like my mother's kind neighbour who was crucial to us at the end. No one could bear to sleep in that house and after we had worked all the first day trying to clear the stuff, we missed the bus. She invited us to stay the night with her. Through her support we were able to use her home as a base; she gave us a wash, and put up butties for us and so on. She was so kind, so diametrically opposite to what my mother had been.

The final twist of the mouse's tail came almost at the end of our clearance. I was looking through the eight carrier bags full of snapshots which my mother had taken during her jaunts. In among some of the happy snaps were blurred photos of mice corpses stretched out on polystyrene food trays, or laid out at the side of a trap.

My Mother's Boyfriend

After her mother began a relationship with a violent boyfriend, Hope's whole family suffered from his brutality. Though she and her brothers and sisters were protected from the worst of his violence, she witnessed many attacks on her mother. Hope's story is therefore also her mother's story, and told to honour the older woman's memory.

Later, when the family was split up, Hope was sent to a succession of children's homes throughout Yorkshire and Nottinghamshire. Though she lives in Liverpool now, she retains many connections with Sheffield, where she lived for some time. Writing about what happened in her childhood has brought many more memories back. 'You feel released,' he says, 'like the chains have gone. Through art and writing I can feel more free.'

Hope's experiences of domestic violence as a child have affected her all her life, and she feels they have been responsible for her suffering physical abuse herself as an adult. 'I have got sucked into abusive relationships also,' she admits. 'Sometimes it is unavoidable.'

The pattern was proving very hard for her to break, but she is beginning to do so, with the support of other Black women in her community.

I sit there staring into the flames of the yesterdays in an old house that doesn't exist in my physical life any more. Again the wood and the coal crack as the fire spits. As it burns alight in the middle of the night my mother gives us toast that has been roasted on the fire. Have you ever heard of roasted toast? I am scared a little. 'Mum, I want to wee wee and I don't want to go upstairs in the dark and the cold of an empty house. It doesn't feel like home any more. What happened? What went wrong, Mum?' I now say in my mind. 'Wee wee in the corner over there...'

What had happened, anyway?

As I remember, I was a little child, very shy, like the rest of my family. Gail was the shyest. She was two years younger than me. Mariella was shy but always spoilt. She was the youngest and fattest and cutest, so really you can understand why. Matthew - he was skinny, always teasing and getting beaten in one way or another. James was a rebellious child, always running away from home and getting into some kind of trouble. He used to put us through many tasks and if we lost or didn't maintain enough strength to go through or win, we were beaten by him. We were all scared of Jamie. He was rough and ready all the time, very intelligent too. I don't think he was scared of anything or anyone. He's changed a little now.

We all shared the same bedroom: four of us. The room couldn't have been more than ten by ten in size. Every wall had a bed pushed tightly up against it, whilst my mother had the other bedroom. There were only two bedrooms and a little landing. We had no bathroom, just a toilet. Now and again the tin bath used to be dragged out, banging all over the place. That's how it was in those times: no tin bath; no bath!

We had a lot of fun in that house. Just a few flashes of good times pass through my mind. Bad times were a usual every day thing when life really got rotten. My mother was very young and had a lot of children to cope with. Sometimes I think she just lived for us. She died when I was thirteen years old after a life of being battered, abused, used, in front of our faces and behind our backs, especially behind the closed doors.

He was a big fellow, about seven foot if I recall correctly. His shoe size was thirteen. They were black like he was. He seemed very humble and calm, but if you listened on the other side of one of those closed doors you wouldn't believe it was the same man, never mind a sane man. He had quite a few nicknames. It's funny because every time one of his names was mentioned people automatically froze or tried to cool themselves, in case they said or did the wrong thing in his presence.

Seven foot six was very big compared to our small childish frames. He was just a boyfriend of my mother's. As my daddy left when we were very tiny, my mother was left with five children. My older sister was taken on holiday when she was born, to Afganistan somewhere, and never came back until 1982, a few months after my mother died. She had a different daddy and it was him who took her away all those years ago. She is now about thirty to thirty-three years old, and I've only ever seen her two times since she came back in 1982.

Anyway, when my mother's boyfriend was in the vicinity everybody knew. He used to have a big car and take us for rides sometimes. Maybe those were some of the good times with him. I remember quite clearly the time I heard screaming and shouting coming from the front room of this same old house. I peered through the key hole and to my horror my mother was being literally strangled, hooked up against the marble table in front of my little, peeping eyes. She was strong and survived. It was just as bad as the time when I witnessed again an act of real terror, when my mother was being pushed head first in the kitchen sink, his large hands strongly and tightly around her head in the water. I never knew why. Surely a human being could avoid such a monstrous performance? Maybe he needed help, just as everybody in our family needed it.

But it didn't stop there. My mother was very strong. We used to sleep in our clothes in the bed, in case he came to the house early in the mornings when it was safe for him, but not safe for us. My mother must have been going through a lot of fear without any help from social or welfare departments. At that time I think the police were out of the question because after she had been to them he would have come back and terrorised my mother even worse. He proved to do so later.

This went on for years. Mother used to cry a lot and tell us how she was fed up. Imagine constant fear and fright; all because the man you used to love wouldn't understand that you wanted to be left in peace to get on with your life, looking after your children. Those nights were some of the worst, especially the unexpected visits when we hadn't put our clothes on to sleep in. We'd have to rush to neighbours or relatives in our nighties, through the back door, whilst he was at the front.

I remember one night it proved almost fatal because we ran out of the house in the usual way and got on a bus. The man we were trying to run away from was on the same bus and when he spotted us he said, 'You can run but you can't hide.' Man, I thought he was going to kill Mum. All I can remember is being very frightened and bright lights on the bus shining and shining. I was tired, hoping it would blow over quickly, maybe even praying that it was all just a bad dream. My poor mother - I think he was pulling her hair tightly or twisting her arms up her back or something. Actually he did break both her arms. Maybe that was the night he did it.

I remember too when her ankle bone, the sharp thing that sticks out of your ankle, was kicked outside in by his foot. She also received stitches to her parts between her legs, busted ear drums, and black eyes, all over a short period of time and she still survived.

Many other things happened to my mother which I call private. Somehow I think those things should be left unspoken. But nonetheless, my dear mother was a very strong, kind caring woman. She always told me she wished she was a bird that could fly away.

Eventually we moved from that old house by about two miles. When I reached the doorstep I remember being sick. I think that may have been one of the times when he had got locked up, but it wasn't too long before our windows were smashed and we were living in fear again. After a while he was locked up again, moving from prison to prison. He did my mother bad. She said that she would haunt him. She also said that he would turn against his mother and end up dead. Both of these things happened.

My mother had a lot of love to offer but the right man wasn't around to receive it at that time, and anyway, we received most of it. She taught us manners, not to swear, not to beg. She was a good mother and even though times were hard she made sure we always had food, clothes and shelter.

Always laughing and singing to us, she started to get sick and ill. She was losing a lot of blood from her body in clots. I remember seeing them in a bowl. Sometimes when I was sleeping she'd go dizzy and faint on my bed. The tears that were shed between us all could have created a reservoir.

Cancer was diagnosed and we were placed in children's homes. I think I went in one first because I became a little hard to handle. After a while my sisters moved back home and were later fostered to my auntie. Sometimes my gran used to look after me. No one would really take me in because I became rebellious a little. My brothers were somewhere else. I can't really remember where, but still, that's another story any way.

I ended up moving from one children's home to another, being called 'Wog' and 'Nigger' and 'Sambo'. It was a nightmare, living with children who never respected Black people, or couldn't spare a thought; children who would stick together and claim to be National Front or part of the Klu Klux Klan.

Many times I was locked up in secure units with a bucket and a bed. I was eleven and twelve years old then. By the time I was thirteen I'd already witnessed most of the abuse that few people have witnessed in a lifetime: staff beating up residents; staff sleeping with residents; staff drawing blood from children; children glue sniffing, petrol sniffing; children putting their hands on anything to get high and take a step from reality; children committing suicide. I personally must have absconded a hundred times to escape my prison-made life.

I ended up sleeping rough, under staircases in a flat, in the bus station cold and hungry, staying in different people's houses just to get a good night's sleep. I ran away to Nottingham, to Ilkeston, and to Chesterfield, Dronfield and Sheffield in South Yorkshire. In Sheffield I had to steal with my friend to fill our hungers.

I made a few friends in Sheffield. Even though I felt free, I still felt trapped, trapped because of the way the system was, trapped because of restrictions, supervision orders, demands, and most of all robbed of a proper childhood and a mother.

Good times only lasted for a short while, but even so, I truly give thanks for them and the good friends I met along the way. Respect to them all!

When I was thirteen my mother passed away after a strong fight. I remember the day. I was just about to leave the children's home, making sure I looked clean and tidy to visit my mother, all boosted up I expect. One of the staff at the children's home told me that they had just received a phone call and that my mother had died. I couldn't believe it. I was lost and absolutely heartbroken, and sad for her.

Somehow I knew it would happen because when I was a child, before I learnt she was sick, I wrote this poem for her:

My Dear Mother

My dear mother was very brave.
  Although I loved her so,
Her heart was broken all the time
  And now she had to go.
I'll never forget that loving face
  As long as I do live.
I loved her so with all my heart
  And all that I could give.

It was read when she had passed on, at the funeral.

I give respect to my mother, for her strength and courage and most of all, her loving kindness. 'We Honour Our Mother...'

She was a good woman.

I finally left residential care when I was fifteen years old, on the condition that I remained under the supervision of a hostel run by Black staff. I welcomed this offer as I seriously needed a break from the children home regime. I was about to become free after, so it seemed, many years of imprisonment. I am not going to knock all of the help I got as a child, because I did get some good help and freedom and experience, in many different ways. No, life is not easy and people are forever making decisions for you. It's like not being able to think for yourself.

I knew if I was placed in a hostel I would be much freer in being able to make my own decisions. I chose, or rather accepted this offer, as my social worker thought it might be better for me too. I also welcomed the idea of the Black and cultural surroundings.

Eventually I moved in and after some time moved out into a flat. This was absolutely wonderful. I adapted straight away to this brand-new experience in my life. I was so happy, so overjoyed; my own decision making, my own sleeping and rising, my own cooking, my own coming in and out as I pleased. I was the perfect house woman, believe it. Everything I owned I cared for and cherished with my heart. This was the life I'd only dreamt of and cried for: to be free.

I met many people and I tried to live a good life. If ever I felt lonely or wanted to turn a few pages back of my past, I'd sit in the park and write poetry; sit by the water and sing songs out of inspiration from the nature that surrounded me. These experiences were so soothing to my soul. From that time I realised I only wanted to be with nature, live as everyone should be living: naturally, free to grow and bloom as the Most High would have planned it. Going to the park became a frequent thing and my songs and poetry became more important to me, as they were the thoughts of my heart and mind.

Finally I placed them all to one side and looked for a job. I did a lot of voluntary work that gave me skills and experience. I was always a quick learner. I started a little work with children aged between two and five years old at a nursery, then I helped as a cook, a sort of youth worker. Afterwards, I took up a job as an assistant chairperson to aid the starving people in Ethiopia. A little after that I had children. This was another new experience. It didn't seem hard at all. I cared for them good. I was very protective towards my children and didn't want any harm to come to them. I didn't even trust a babysitter. These children were mine, something to call my own, my own flesh and blood and nobody was going to take them away from me. I love them.

Sometimes me and their daddy would argue, but who doesn't? We tried reasoning, a kind of agreement more than an argument. This would work in many cases but due to emotions and feelings that tend to grow on you throughout the years, this didn't solve things. I started to get abused. Maybe I was still young in my thinkings and doings. We are not all perfect, but trying really counts. I'd try to be the perfect mother and wife, even though I wasn't married at the time in society's way. We were living together and I started to receive a few beatings like my mother would have done, but not quite as drastic. These were shrugged off after a while. That relationship was shrugged off after a while too.

I left and moved to a different town, and became a free woman again, this time a little shaky about things and people. I began to live a more shielded life, being careful who I was with in any kind of relationship, whether it was business or friendship, or a more close kind of relationship. Being on this kind of guard protected me but sometimes my kindness and generosity grew until I was helping people more than I was helping myself. Of course advantage was taken of me, but I just tried to be more moderate with things. I learned all about people and the way they lived. I tried to help them if I could and teach them about some of the good things in life that I knew of. After a while I started to get into drama and writing and anything to do with performance that came my way.

And this is what I do now at the age of twenty-six. This story is a part of my work. Maybe one day you will be able to read my poems and learn what I have learned in my life time, away from that cold empty house of memories, that was also our safe house when there was nowhere to go, or nowhere to run. There are other houses in these times where many try to live a peaceful life, but are being dominated by some kind of force from someone who has power.

You determine your own destiny! Think carefully before making moves in your life.

I finish with one of the songs I have written:

Let's live together now
and try to be as one,
love is forever;
there's a battle to be won.
Brothers and sisters
let us try to unify,
have faith in the Father
and you shall never die.

Let's live together now
Let you and I praise the Most High,
and look to the future;
let's rejoice with love and try.
The hotter the battle
the sweeter the victory.
Reward time is coming now;
just judgement you shall see.

Let's live together now
in love and harmony,
and let us find happiness
in peace and unity.
Listen all you children,
arm your soul and seek your goal.
Hear the words of the Father;
Sing of the promise
that is being retold.

The Honour of the Regiment

As he recovers from a serious illness, Christian is bringing a prosecution against his father, who abused him from the time he was eighteen months old, until he was twenty. Publishing his story is a way of 'closing the event' and a final revenge.

Describing himself and his background, Christian wrote:

I was asked to include a small piece about me to go before my story.

My name is Christian, and I am who I am.

I am proud of what I have become, out of a shell of self-destructiveness.

Who I am does not matter to other people, only to me.

I sit here in hospital writing this story so that you will understand what happened and why I hurt all those I loved and lost.

I am fighting a battle against cancer, yet another legacy given to me by my father.

For the last five years my life has been a living hell. I changed my name, my family and my whole background, and for what? I felt ashamed. I felt lower than anything you could imagine.

In my life I have been a thief, a prostitute and a very successful person in business, and all before my twenty-sixth birthday.

Now as I sit writing this I have an uncanny feeling of lightness on my conscience. For me it is over. The truth is out and a prosecution is in the future.

The police interviewed me on video in my hospital room for three hours. I realise they tried all sorts of psychological tricks to check whether I was telling the truth. I felt 'done in' afterwards, but the past is out of my system now. What happened, happened, and it is gone from me. The Special Investigation Branch of the army police have taken up the case and there is to be a military prosecution of my father, five years after the event. They tell me I am the first male victim to bring a case so long after the last incident.

People have finally listened to what I have had to say to them. The man who ruined my life, my father, will finally pay for what he has done to me - twenty years of physical, mental and sexual abuse, culminating in an act of rape when I was twenty years old and the most brutal beating which left me in hospital for eight weeks. Six of those weeks I was in intensive care, with dedicated staff trying to save my life.

It was that last act against my person that caused me the most mental damage of all; it is the one I relive every time I have sex with somebody. I have never made love, I don't know what love is. How could I? In our house there was only hatred. Love is very pure and innocent.

I was first raped when I was eighteen months old. The abuse continued until I was twenty, except for a short break while I was away. As I look back on the last act of rape and think about the physical pain I had to endure during and after, I shudder. I almost died from it. My face was smashed into a wall until it was almost indistinguishable, with most of it broken. My ribs were broken. I was kicked in the stomach until I had severe internal bleeding, and then subjected to four and a half hours of sex.

Every time I go for treatment for my cancer I think of that ordeal, because that is how I developed it. The doctors have told me it was a major contributory factor. My face was reconstructed by an eminent cosmetic surgeon, but my stomach will never be repaired.

I often think of the word 'father' and what it means really. A father is somebody you should be proud of, somebody who sets you a good example, somebody who is firm not cruel. That may be what your description of a father is, but it is not mine. It is the father I invented for myself in the last five years. In reality my father was evil, cruel, sardonic, a man who when he came in from work would kick me out of the way if I was in the direct line of fire, or just knock me down. A man who took the greatest pleasure in throwing me through a plate glass window because I didn't move fast enough, or when he needed sexual gratification, would use me like a cheap sex aid.

I often asked myself why, or would think, 'If only I had done things differently.' I grew up first believing this was a normal family situation, and later I thought it was my fault. If I could become a better son, maybe he would like me more?

I know different now. Such situations were not normal. It was not my fault, and no matter what I did for him, my father would never change.

I won't describe what he did to me as you have read it a thousand times in your daily papers. These situations are just many of the unfortunate things in life. You have read them and know that it happens. What you probably don't know is the after-effects that these situations cause.

I am twenty-five years old now and have only just learnt that it does not matter what you are. People like you because you are you, not for what you've got or what you can give them. It has taken me five long years to realise this, after many years of hurting people before they hurt me.

After I left home at the age of twenty, I went to live in Berlin. I had a new start, a new face and a good education. I had a little money but not a lot. I had to steal food to eat and became a prostitute to pay the rent. I changed my name because I was named after my father. I invented a whole new life for myself and started to live a lie - a lie that almost destroyed me. Every relationship I had never worked. Every time we had sex I felt dirty. I still do.

Even when I reported what was happening to me to the various people that you see recommended, teachers, police or some other responsible adult, it was ignored or lost in the files. Something to do with the honour of the regiment and all that jazz! There was a whitewash to protect the army. I laid a complaint and it was ignored. The German civil police closed ranks when they found it was a British Army case. When I phoned the abuse hot line I was told to ring the Gay Switchboard. 'But I'm not gay,' I said. They replied that they only dealt with females. I felt despondent and rejected, with nowhere to turn.

Things are different now. If it had not been for the fact that I almost died a few weeks ago, I would have gone on living a lie. I lay there in a hospital room thinking about what my life meant and what I had done to my good friend - in fact the only person who was a real friend to me - and all the hurt I had caused him.

Prior to my emergency entrance into the infirmary, we had had a big argument. We actually came to blows in the middle of the town centre. It took a long time for us to start talking again afterwards, and a lot of water has gone under the bridge.

He has come to the hospital every day, and stayed with me all day until eleven o'clock at night. He has pulled me through the cancer and has stood by me. I have a lot to thank him for, and will probably never be able to repay him for what he has done.

If it was not for him, none of this would have ever come out and I would have gone on hurting people.

He has taught me the meaning of the word dignity. I am a person in my own right and worth as much as anybody else.

A Sense of Living

Joanne and Abby wanted to tell their stories jointly. They first met when they attended an Incest Survivors' group at the Bradford Rape Crisis Centre. Both had been abused as children by members of their own family: Joanne by her grandfather, Abby by an uncle.

Over the next few months the two became friends. Since then their friendship has deepened, and has sustained them as they have come to terms with the effect of abuse on their lives. Ultimately they decided they wanted to help other women with similar experiences to their own, and after taking the necessary training together, became counsellors with the Bradford Rape Crisis Centre - 'once just a dream ' - as Joanne put it. Having had counselling themselves at the centre, they have 'come full circle.'

Now both are hoping to use their experiences in new careers. Abby is a nurse, but she is also a student - something she never thought she would be - taking a Community Studies Degree course at a local college. For her, she says, college is work; nursing pays the bills. When she is qualified, she hopes to be employed in the voluntary sector, helping women survivors of violence.

Joanne is a civil servant, and already serves as Sexual Harassment Officer for her workplace. She too is studying part-time, taking a course in Psychology. Next year she will move on to Bradford University to begin a degree in the Social Sciences, specialising in Psychology. Ultimately she hopes to run her own counselling service, and is at present writing a book recounting her experience of childhood abuse.

Sitting in the office at the Bradford Rape Crisis Centre, the two women began by recalling how difficult they found it as children to disclose what was happening to them. Joanne begins their story.

Joanne

For six years I was sexually abused by my grandfather. My earliest memories are of when I was four years old, but it may have been happening before then. I have no memories of anything before that age, so I can't say. I kept it secret. No one ever knew. I swore to myself that I would never tell anyone - I felt that it would all be alright if I didn't. I felt it was all my fault and that as long as I kept my mouth shut I would be OK. It never occurred to me that my grandfather would want to keep it quiet. I used to worry that he would say something.

I coped with it because my family life was brilliant, and what was happening with my grandad didn't seem so destructive to me. I didn't really know it didn't go on elsewhere. I was too young to understand what was going on or that it was wrong, and I was blackmailed into loads of things.

My father died when I was ten and the abuse stopped then. His family blamed my mother for allowing him to die - as if she could have stopped it - and abandoned us. I used to pray that something would come along to stop what my grandfather was doing, and when it did it was the death of my dad.

I was devastated. I had loved my dad more than anyone in the world and had kept quiet about what was happening to keep his love. Grandad used to use that as an argument, 'Keep it quiet or they won't love you any more...'

My world came crashing down. I had lost my father's love anyway. Yet I still didn't talk about what had been going on. I didn't trust anyone enough. I was so unsure about every single thing, I felt I had to carry on the way I used to, keeping my mouth shut.

At the age of ten you start to understand what is going on around you - sex and so on - and I needed someone to talk to, but I couldn't get support from my own family. My mother's life was so bad with Dad gone, our roles had reversed. In my own mind Mum was like a little child and I was like her mother. I was supporting her and I couldn't dump everything onto her. Nor could I say anything to the rest of the family or to my teachers, because it would get back to my mother. There was no one in the world who could act to help me. Even later on I didn't let my mother know what had gone on. I just felt I was different from others, and alone, and that I had lost everything. I couldn't remember life without being abused.

So I carried on. It was only when I was leaving school that I had a chance to get away from everything I knew, to make a new life and become a new person. I started a job and got on really well. I thought I didn't have a problem in the world, that I had made myself into a completely different person to what I'd been.

Then they moved me at work, after I had been in the one place for two years and got to know everyone. It was just a simple move but that move brought everything to a sudden halt for me, and led me to a breakdown. It was as though I had fought again and lost again. I wasn't strong enough to cope another time.

By then I was aged twenty-one. It all just erupted; I couldn't do anything at all and got into a very depressive state, unable to make any decision. I wanted to die - I couldn't stand the thought of being like I was any more.

Because of my depression I had to have a few weeks off sick from work. That was what made me finally speak up. I was hiding from everyone, from work and from my family, still lying and still keeping up the pretence that I was someone I wasn't, but I had to go to my doctor to get a sick note. While I was there I told her about what had happened with my grandfather.

The doctor sent me for therapy at hospital, and I had quite a lot of sessions with them. Then I was put in contact with the Rape Crisis Centre. They had an Incest

Survivors' group where I could meet other women who had had a similar experience. It took me a lot of courage to go. I was sure they were just going to put me away.

The start of everything was walking through this door and hearing other women saying what I wanted to say myself. I didn't believe anyone else could have been through what I had. By listening to others talking and seeing that they were not struck down for doing so, I began to learn to express what I was feeling myself. Knowing I was normal made an enormous difference.

At that time I was still attending therapy at hospital, and one to one counselling here.

Abby and I met that first day. I was really scared. It was still really important to me that no one knew, that no one in the family should find out. My biggest fear was of walking into the group and seeing someone I knew. I remember walking towards the door and knowing people were sitting in here waiting, and having to force myself to come in. Abby was sitting by the door. I couldn't look at her at first. I looked everywhere except at her. I needed to know she was there but I couldn't look at her. It was all very uncomfortable - just awful. I never wanted friendship out of the group, not even to get to know people. I wanted to go back after the meeting and live my life as I should be living it, to just walk away.

Yet we ended up finding we had so much in common because of what we had both gone through, that we became really good friends. We helped each other through set-backs. There was no pressure there. We could act and say what we wanted and cry if we wanted, knowing the other wouldn't think anything about it.

We both got help, and people were there to help us when we needed it, but they could never understand fully because they were not survivors themselves. You can't fully understand unless you've been there. That was partly why we decided to ask to become counsellors ourselves.

When you leave a support group you do it because you feel the group can no longer help you. You are making your own steps and need time to see if you can do so. We had a year to wait before we could start training, as the Centre only recruits every so often. We both felt we needed that year.

By keeping it quiet all that time it comes back and knocks you flying. Now I'm not running away any more. I used to want it to just go away - to walk out on it, but now I know it will always be a part of me. I'm proud I can survive. I can accept the fact that it happened and things will never be any different. It's nice to think that in some strange way I'm lucky. I've come to understand myself. So many people never have the chance to know themselves.

I'm still definite that I don't want all my family to know about it. I used to talk to work colleagues and they would say 'Get out of it; stop hanging on to it,' but I want it to be part of my life. I want to work with it, to ask 'Why was it me?' I have to feel there was a purpose to it happening, that perhaps it was so that I could help others.

I can't get back at my grandad because he died. His death was what I had wanted because of my fear that he would say something about what he'd done. When I heard he was dead I was so relieved; I felt I was safe. But it just hasn't worked out like that. Now I'm angry that I didn't do something about it at the time. I've got enough strength now. If he was alive now I would prosecute.

It was always so important that my family didn't know, but now I've managed to tell my mum. I thought she would think so badly of me she would be against me. It took me a hell of a long time to do it. It wasn't planned and it was probably the wrong way to say it, in an argument, but I'm no longer living a lie. I don't talk about it with Mum - she was angry I never trusted her enough to tell her, and very upset about it all. I can't give

104

her the support she wants. Maybe that's cold but I can't do otherwise. I had to survive on my own and I can't allow her to step in now. It's too late. She wasn't there when I needed her; she had her own things then.

Maybe that will all change though some time. You never stop working on yourself. As the years go by you are changing all the time. You don't know what's coming until it does. I can handle such changes now; I couldn't before. I had no strength, not enough pride or good feeling about myself to fight.

I remember one exercise we had in the group. We had to write down twelve things that we liked about ourselves before we were allowed to leave. I was furious. I'd been going through real shit saying why I hated myself. I can laugh about it now but at the time I couldn't believe the arrogance of someone asking for twelve things I liked. I was so annoyed, yet that was the very thing that made me fight. By the time I came to leave I could write down twelve things. That exercise helped me to change.

Dad wasn't close to his relatives, though he was always close to his own family, that is to his wife and children. Mum told me he never trusted his father enough to leave Mum with him, but he left his children - because you never thought such things could happen. It's nice to know Dad didn't think his father was such a wonderful person after all, though it makes me angry that I never knew that at the time.

There are men you can trust. I really do believe that. It's wrong of the media to make you suspicious of them all. I want all children to have as happy and close a relationship with their fathers as I had.

I can remember now quite clearly what my grandfather used to do. At the time you know it's wrong but you don't understand why it is. You really believe it's your fault. You have an internal dread someone's going to find out what you've done. Even now I get flashbacks.

The slightest thing will bring it back. You can never wipe it away. Smells, colours, feelings will trigger memories. A material that used to be on the bed - everytime I see that material it's immediately just there in front of me.

You literally have to start trusting in people again, believing in people. If someone knows you've been abused they immediately think it's your father. I loved my father. I don't hate men, because my father was a man and I loved him. He would never ever have abused me. I have difficulty understanding some survivors who do hate men. It's just one man I hate. I find it hard to live with the fact that if I had spoken up my family would have stood by me.

I'm not afraid to show my emotions now. For far too long I pretended to feel things I didn't. I'm not willing to do it any more. It's important for me to recognise for myself that all parts of me centre on a particular instance - that everything that happened is part of what you are. Nobody ever talked about such things when I was young. Some women will never mention it even now.

I'm still angry my grandfather got away with it. But sometimes I'm relieved that it happened the way that it did. I never had to put Dad into a position where he had to choose between me and his father. Sometimes I feel both of them are still around, and I wonder, 'Are they together? How is their relationship now?' I like to feel there are things after death, though I don't have any idea of Heaven up there and Hell down there. I wouldn't be angry if they were together - that Dad still loves his father. What is important is that my dad loves me. In a way I want my grandfather to be around so that he knows what I'm doing and that he hasn't crushed me.

You're sorry enough for yourself - you don't need others to be sorry. One of the really beautiful things is you really do want to die, and then you really want to live. Others don't have this sense of living, of being completely alive.

106

Abby

It was my uncle who raped me, when I was thirteen. We used to go on holiday in Somerset to stay with him. I was abused for a week, not for years, but it had a very bad effect on me. I can still remember sitting on the train afterwards telling myself I wouldn't have to see my uncle again for another two years, and trying to put what had happened out of my head.

Three months later my dad died. On one level I thought, 'Brilliant! Now we won't have to go and see his relatives again.' It also gave me a really valid reason why I should be so upset.

I started pushing it all down because of Dad's death. I had been very close to my father. For three years I had no recollection of what my uncle had done - I had pushed it down so deep I didn't think it had happened. Then when I was sixteen and a half I was rushed into hospital with appendicitis. Being in hospital brought it all back - people prodding about with my body. I ended up breaking down one day and telling my mum.

Mum was very good about it for three months, but after that she started to say I mustn't let it ruin my life. So I pushed it down again, to make her think I was happy.

Later I got into a relationship which was quite violent. I moved to Bradford just before it broke up. I came to counselling because of the violence of that relationship and began to realise the effect the earlier abuse had had on my life. Like Jo I had wanted to be a new person, someone I wasn't.

When I first came here to the Centre I was just numb. I didn't know how to cry. I just didn't know how to feel anything. For two years I came to one-to-one counselling. Gradually I started building my life again, getting in touch with myself and my feelings, learning to cry. My counsellor invited me to join the Incest

Survivors' group. Part of me didn't want to meet people, part did.

The day I started the group was really weird. I went to the police in the morning and was there for five hours, making a statement about what my uncle had done to me. That was the start of me moving on and stopping looking back to the past. Afterwards, I came to the group. The week after that I changed my name. I had got control of my life at last. There was still a lot I had to work on, but I'd made steps towards believing in a future.

I remember Jo joining the group that first day. I kept getting quick glances from her. It took a few months, then we realised we had so much else in common beside our experience. We used to meet up and talk and talk and talk.

I was in the group for six or seven months and then I left. Joanne was carrying on in it, but we used to meet still and talk about what was going on and what we wanted to happen. We found we both wanted to work at the Centre - I'd been thinking about it for some time. We knew they wouldn't want us to start straight away, but we came along and talked about it together.

The months after you leave a group are the most important of all, like the first year after you take your driving test. Everything of that time comes back to you. You know you can ring the Centre if necessary, but you don't want to because you'll feel you've failed. I felt I needed to prove what had happened to me wasn't affecting my life now - to prove that I could live on my own.

It was really important to me that I went to the police - that my uncle was questioned in the cells and that the family and all his neighbours knew. He pleaded not guilty all the way through but the police were on my side after they'd talked to him. That was brilliant. The case didn't go to court though. The Crown Prosecution thought I wouldn't be able to stand it, even though my mother and brother had made statements about things I'd forgotten and there was a lot of evidence. The police would have taken it to court if it had been left to them. At the time I was angry, but now I feel everybody knows and that's enough. Making my statement moved me on. I feel I've got back at him.

Mum said afterwards that she never liked my uncle - never felt comfortable with him. It makes it easier for me to know that. He was a creep. Yet before it happened he meant a lot to me.

It's what you turn your experience into - whether you can turn it into something positive. I wouldn't be the person I am if I hadn't been through counselling. It's really paid off for me. I've never put so much into anything.

I will show my emotions now. I didn't cry for six years. I saw really awful things and didn't cry. I can still remember the first time I cried - the sense of all this pressure going. It was really amazing. I feel like I need to say to people, 'I'm really strong now, really assertive, proud of who I am.' It's hard though. Ninety-nine per cent of the time I feel good but there are still times when I feel sad - sad rather than bad. Every six months or so, rather than twenty-four hours a day, seven days a week as it used to be.

I have a fear of being sympathised with, people saying 'poor thing'. I don't want sympathy; I want people to know why I am as I am, not so they can feel sorry for me.

There are more places now where you can talk, and there's less of a taboo because of the media, but for women it's still very difficult. I don't think I could have talked about it earlier, even if it was like today and easier.

The most important issue to me now is violence against women. It's really, really important to me that people should know about it and that I should work with women who have experienced violence, like myself. I suppose it's a way of getting back at my uncle, of saying, 'Stuff you! I've become stronger, better, more assertive because of it. Whatever you tried, it hasn't worked!'

The key is getting control - regaining control over your own life. I never thought of myself as a survivor. It's nice now to realise it, and say, 'I am a survivor. Every day that passes I'm surviving still! I am going to survive!'

DIRECTORY

The following list is not exhaustive! If you come across sources of help not included, pass the word around. At present it is very difficult to find out what is available and new groups are appearing all the time.

Phone numbers, opening hours and addresses change regularly too, as groups respond to changes in staff or funding. By the time you read this, some details may well be out of date. Hopefully however, the contact given here will pass you on to the right person.

Keep trying. Support is available in many forms, from both professionals and volunteers (many of whom are survivors themselves).

NATIONAL SOURCES OF HELP

FOR ADULTS

CHILD ABUSE SURVIVOR NETWORK
To receive information on their services, send a stamped addressed envelope to:

PO Box 1, London N17 SN
Telephone 071 278 8414

FAMILY WELFARE ASSOCIATION

Call 071 254 6251 for details

HEALTH SERVICE
Your GP can put you in touch with specialist consultants or paediatricians locally, who will offer advice and consultations if needed.

MIND
If you are still feeling badly upset by what happened, MIND can offer information on mental health matters. Many local associations run day centres and drop-in facilities. The national contact is:

Granta House,15-19 Broadway, Stratford, London E15 4BQ
Telephone 081 519 2122

NATIONAL COUNCIL FOR ONE PARENT FAMILIES
They provide a range of information leaflets and booklets. No advice is given.

Telephone 071 267 1361 for details

POLICE

The police are now setting up special Domestic Violence Units with staff trained to deal sensitively with women and children suffering physical abuse. They also have women officers you can talk to in cases of rape or sexual assault. Contact the unit which covers your area. Your local police station will give you the number. In cases of immediate danger phone 999.

RELATE

Experiencing marital or relationship problems because of past abuse? It may help to contact your local branch of Relate. The national address is:

Herbert Grey College, Little Church Sreet, Rugby CV21 3AP
Telephone 0788 573241

(THE) SAMARITANS

Ring The Samaritans at any time of the day or night if you are feeling really desperate. Their local number is in every telephone book. The Administrative Head Office is:

10 The Grove, Slough, Berks SL1 1QP
Telephone 0753 532713 (Not a helpline)

SANELINE

Saneline is a national telephone helpline providing support and information to people suffering from mental health problems, their families, friends and professionals. It is open 2.00 pm to midnight every day of the year.

Saneline 071 724 8000

SCHOOLS

Head teachers can make confidential referrals to Social Services or the Health Service if there is concern about a child in the school's care. Nowadays teachers are given guidance about what to do if a child talks about abuse to them, and teachers are sometimes the first to notice signs of abuse. If you are still at school, don't hesitate to have a chat to a teacher you feel you can trust.

SOCIAL SERVICES

There are advice sessions and groups in many Social Service areas. Contact your Neighbourhood Office through the Duty Social Work System. The local telephone directory will include the number, usually listed under City Council entries.

VICTIM SUPPORT SCHEMES

These are developing in a number of cities, and train volunteers to support victims of crime. They are separate to the police, though work closely with them. If there is no Rape Crisis Line or Domestic Violence Unit in your area, a local Victim Support Scheme might be able to help you. The police will have the number and it will also be in local directories. In Leeds for example, there are three schemes, covering the city.

WOMEN'S AID
If you need to leave home due to physical, emotional or sexual abuse, Women's Aid can give you and your children a safe place to stay and confidential information and advice.

National Emergency Helpline 0272 633542
Open 10.00 am - 4.00 pm, Monday to Friday.
There is an answerphone service at all other times.

PARTICULARLY FOR CHILDREN AND YOUNG PEOPLE

ADVICE, ADVOCACY AND REPRESENTATION SERVICE FOR CHILDREN (ASC)
Provides a confidential service for children and young people who need and receive services from Social Services Departments. Ring between 4.00 pm and 10.00 pm.

1 Sickle Street, Manchester,
Freephone 0800 616101

BLACK AND IN CARE

William Morris Community Centre, Greenleaf Road, Walthamstow, London E17 6QQ.
Not on the telephone.

CHILDLINE
Childline offers a twenty-four hour national telephone counselling service to children and young people in trouble, need or danger. The service is free and confidential. Childen can also write to Childline at

Freepost 1111, London N1 0BR.
Telephone 0800 1111

CHILDREN'S LEGAL CENTRE

20 Compton Terrace, London N1 2UN, Telephone 071 359 6251
Advice line 2.00 pm - 5.00 pm, Mondays to Fridays.

(THE) CHILDREN'S RIGHTS OFFICERS' ASSOCIATION

5th Floor, National Deposit House, 1 Eastgate, Leeds LS2 7LY
No phone

INDEPENDENT REPRESENTATION FOR CHILDREN IN NEED

23a Hawthorne Drive, Heswall, Wirral, Merseyside L61 6UP
Telephone 051 342 7852

NSPCC CHILD PROTECTION LINE
Twenty-four hour freephone service. Advice and counselling for anyone involved in or concerned about abuse to children, including children themselves.

Telephone 0800 800500

OMBUDSMAN
For complaints about local authorities contact the Local Government Ombudsman who covers your area:

North of England and North Midlands:
Beverley House, 17 Shipton Road, York YO3 6FZ
Telephone 0904 630151

East Anglia, the South West, the West, the South and Central England:
The Oaks, Westwood Way, Westwood Business Park, Coventry CV4 8JB
Telephone 0203 695999

The Rest of England:
21 Queen Anne's Gate, London SW1H 9BU
Telephone 071 915 3210

Wales:
Derwen House, Court Road
Bridgend, Mid Glamorgan CF31 1BN
Telephone 0656 661325

THE ADVOCACY UNIT, THE CHILDREN'S SOCIETY
Provides advice and information to young people in South Wales. Follow-up support service can be provided only to children and young people who are looked after by South Glamorgan Social Services.

14 Cathedral Road, Cardiff CF1 9LJ
Telephone 0222 396974

WHO CARES TRUST

Ring for advice and help. They may be able to give you a local contact.

Telephone 071 833 9047

YOUNG MINDS

Young Minds can tell you about local mental health services for children, young people and their families.

22a Boston Place, London NW1 6ER.
Telephone 071 724 7262

OTHER SOURCES OF HELP YOU MIGHT NEED

AIDS

National Aids Helpline:
Provides advice about HIV and AIDS, twenty four hours a day. All calls are free from anywhere in the UK. Help is offered in the following languages:-

Bengali, Gujarati, Hindi, Punjabi, Urdu and English:
0800 282445, 6.00 pm - 10.00 pm, Wednesdays

Cantonese and English:
0800 282446, 6.00 pm - 10.00 pm, Tuesdays

Arabic and English:
0800 282447, 6.00 pm - 10.00 pm, Wednesdays

A minicom is available for the hearing impaired
on 0800 521361, 10.00 am - 10.00 pm daily.

Many cities now have their own AIDS/HIV advice lines and support groups. Look in the local phone book, or ask at your health centre. The National Aids Helpline will also give you advice on local resources.

ADDICTION

There are Addiction Units or similar sources of help for drug users in many towns. See the local list for examples in West Yorkshire.

ALCOHOLICS ANONYMOUS (AA)

Are you drinking too heavily? Contact your local branch of the AA for support. Social Services or The Samaritans should have the number. There is also a listing under 'AA' in every phone directory. AA will put you in touch with a recovering alcoholic to talk to on a one-to-one basis.

AL-ANON/ALATEEN
For family and friends of alcoholics.
They will put anyone who rings in touch with local contacts and group
meeting places.

National contact number: 071 4030888 (Twenty-four hour helpline).

BHAN (Black HIV/AIDS Network)
The Drop-In Centre is open from 10.00 am - 5.00 pm, Monday to Friday.
Counselling is available in Hindi, Urdu, Gujarati, Punjabi and Kiswahli.
Counselling can also be arranged in Thai, Vietnamese, Bengali, Amharic,
Punjabi, Cantonese, Arabic and Chinese dialects.

Administrative Office:
First Floor, Saint Stephen's House, 41 Uxbridge Road, London W12 8LH
Telephone 081 749 2828

Drop-In Centre:
111 Devonport Road, London W12 8PB
Telephone 081 742 9049

BLACKLINERS HELPLINE
Offers support for people of African, Caribbean and Asian descent
affected by HIV and AIDS.

Unit 46, Eurolink Business Centre, 49 Effra Road, London SW2 1BZ
Helpline 071 738 5274.

BODY POSITIVE LONDON
A helpline is available on 071 373 9124, 7.00 pm - 10.00 pm every
evening. Body Positive provides a free newsletter, hardship grants, social
centre, penpal service and London based support groups for men and
women who are HIV Positive or closely affected.

51b Philbeach Gardens, London SW5 9EB
Telephone 071 835 1045

CITIZEN'S ADVICE BUREAUX
The CAB can often offer advice on where to seek help with legal matters,
or give you contact numbers for local agencies and groups. Ask at your
library for the venue and times of your nearest sessions.

DRUGS AND SOLVENTS LITERATURE

BAPS, Health Publications Unit, DSS Distribution Centre
Heywood Stores, Manchester Road, Heywood, Lancashire OL10 2PZ
Telephone free on 0800 555777

EATING DISORDERS ASSOCIATION

If you want an opportunity to talk in confidence to someone who understands the problems of anorexia and bulimia, ring the telephone helpline: 0603 621414, 9 am - 6.30 pm Monday to Friday.
There is also a Youth helpline (Eighteen years and under): 0603 765050, 4.00 pm - 6.00pm, Monday, Tuesday and Wednesday.
The EDA counsellor will ring young people back to save them the cost of the call.
A recorded message can be heard on 0336 420568. Calls cost 37p per minute cheap rate and 49p at other times.

Sackville Place,
44 Magdalen Street,
Norwich, Norfolk NR3 1JU
Telephone 0603 621414

LONDON LESBIAN AND GAY SWITCHBOARD

Telephone 071 837 7324

MAINLINERS

Provides support for people affected by HIV and drugs.

205 Stockwell Road,
London SW9 9FL.
Telephone 071 737 3141

NATIONAL COUNCIL FOR ONE PARENT FAMILIES

There is no advice line, but publications and information leaflets are free to lone parents.

Telephone 071 267 1361

NATIONAL FEDERATION OF SOLO CLUBS

Telephone 021 236 2879

POSITIVELY WOMEN

5 Sebastian Street, London EC1V OHE
Telephone 071 490 5515 (Client services)
A helpline is available
Monday to Friday,
12.00 noon - 2.00 pm.
Telephone 071 490 2327.

THE TERRENCE HIGGINS TRUST

The Terrence Higgins Trust provides practical support, help, counselling and advice for anyone with or concerned about, AIDS and HIV infection. It also offers a wide range of other services which are open to all gay men. Gay male counsellors, buddies and helpline volunteers are available on request. Support for drug users (including those in prison) is offered.

52-54 Grays Inn Road, London WC1X 8JU
Telephone 071 831 0330
Helpline 071 242 1010,
12.00 noon - 10.00 pm, daily.

WEST YORKSHIRE AND SURROUNDING AREA

Groups marked 'W' are for women only. Those with an 'M' beside them are for male survivors. The rest are available to both sexes.

ACT

Act can only accept referrals for counselling through Wakefield Clinical Psychology Primary Care Services. It is based at Pinderfields Hospital. Talk to your GP about this service.

ADDICTION
Bradford:

The Bridge Project, 2nd Floor, Equity Chambers,
40 Picadilly, Bradford BD1 3NN
Telephone 0274 723863
10.00 am - 4.30 pm Monday to Friday.

Keighley:
Project 6, 11-13 Temple Street, Keighley BD21 2AD
Telephone 0535 610180
9.00 am - 4.45 pm, Monday, Tuesday, Thursday and Friday;
12.00 pm - 8.00 pm Wednesdays.

Sheffield:
Rockingham Drug Project, 17 Rockingham Street, Sheffield S1 4EB
Advice Line: 0742 580033

ALCOHOLICS ANONYMOUS

Oxford Place Methodist Church, Oxford Place, Leeds
Telephone 0532 454567

BRADFORD RAPE CRISIS (W)

Free and confidential counselling service run by women for women and girls, who have been raped or sexually abused. They also run Incest Survivors' groups.

Telephone 0274 308270

LEEDS CRISIS CENTRE

Contact your GP or social worker for a referral if you need advice or counselling in a crisis, or phone direct.
The Centre only provides short term counselling, up to a maximum of eight weeks.

Telephone 0532 755898

LEEDS GAY SWITCHBOARD

Offers advice, information and support on all topics related to lesbians and gay men.

Telephone 0532 453588 daily 7.00 pm - 10.00 pm except
Tuesdays,when calls are answered by Lesbian Line, 7.30 - 9.30 pm.

LEEDS INCEST PROJECT (W)

LIP is run by women for women and girls who have been or are being sexually abused by someone in a position of power or trust. They will support:
girls who are being, or have been, sexually abused;
girls and women who are supporting or coming to terms with the abuse of, for example, a child, sister, or friend;
girls and women needing practical support i.e. doctors, courts and housing.
LIP offers face-to-face counselling, both individiually and in groups. If there are no spaces, there may be a waiting list or LIP can refer you to another organisation they work with.

c/o Leeds Rape Crisis Centre, P.O. Box 27 Wellington Street
Leeds LS2 7EG
Telephone 0532 440058/441323
Strictly confidential.

LEEDS MIND

Provides information regading mental health problems, Day and Drop-In Centres.

82 Cardigan Road, Leeds LS6 3BJ
Telephone 0532 307608

LEEDS RAPE CRISIS CENTRE (W)

Leeds Rape Crisis Centre is run by women for women and girls who have been raped, sexually assaulted or harrassed - whether by a friend, stranger, partner, workmate, acquaintance, neighbour, or relative (man or woman). It aims to provide a service which is accessible to all women, regardless of race, class, disability, sexuality or age, including all women involved in prostitution.

The Centre provides a twenty-four hour answerphone service staffed by trained volunteers and part-time staff, and additional support as requested by women, such as police visits, face-to-face counselling etc. Initial contact is by telephone. There is no limit to users' length of stay / involvement and the service is free and confidential.

Leeds Rape Crisis Centre also runs a rape survivors group and an Incest Survivors' group.

P.O. Box 27, Wellington Street, Leeds LS2 7EG
Telephone 0532 441323 (office) or 440058 (Crisis Line).
Call 0532 441323 if you are hearing impaired.

LESBIAN LINE (LEEDS) (W)

Tuesdays, 7.30 pm - 9.30 pm
Telephone 0532 453588,

LISA (W)

Leeds Incest Survivors Action

LISA provides a confidential telephone counselling line and confidential face to face counselling. It is a service run by women child sexual abuse survivors, for survivors.

P.O. Box 27, Leeds LS2 7EG
Telephone 0532 310949

MESMAC

(Men Who Have Sex With Men Action In The Community) (M)
Provides community based health initiatives for gay men and men who have sex with men; outreach work in pubs and clubs; street work; various groups, including Rent Boy Action, Gay Men's Health Group and Black Gay Men's Group.

Bradford: 0274 395815
Leeds Area: 0532 444209
Wakefield: 0924 814400
Newcastle: 091 233 1333

THE MEN'S ROOM (M)

Free condoms, information and advice on men's health; staffed by a male nurse.

Burmantofts Health Centre, Cromwell Mount, Leeds LS9 7ST
Telephone 0532 484330

NIGHTSTOP (BARNARDOS) PROJECT

If you are between sixteen and twenty-five years old, single and have left home, Nightstop may be able to find you accommodation for the night in the home of a volunteer. They do not take self-referrals, only via another agency, including Social Services, Housing Departments, CAB etc.

Leeds:
53 Cardigan Lane, Burley, Leeds LS4 2LE

Bradford:
5 Wilmer Drive, Heaton, Bradford BD9 4AR

Wakefield:
Wakefield Accommodation Project, c/o Flanshaw Children's Centre
6, Springfield Grange, Flanshaw, Wakefield WF2 9QP

PERSON TO PERSON

Offers a 'listening post' for people who are anxious, worried or distressed. Where appropriate, on-going listening service and support is provided, or a referral is made to another agency able to assist.
The service is available from 10.00 am to 2.00 pm Monday to Friday and is staffed by a team of experienced volunteer counsellors.

Oxford Place Centre, Oxford Place, Leeds 1
Telephone 0532 453502

POLICE DOMESTIC VIOLENCE AND CHILD PROTECTION UNITS

All units have an answerphone service. Interpreters are available.
In cases of immediate danger call 999.

Bradford: (Two units shortly to amalgamate into one)
0274 373154 and 0274 376061
Calder Valley: 0422 375700
Huddersfield: 0484 436661
Leeds: North (Horsforth) 0532 395042
East (Millgarth) 0532 413089
South (Morley)   0532 382062
Freephone advice line 0800 181504
Wakefield: 0924 293350

(LEEDS) RELATE COUNSELLING SERVICE

Relate can provide marriage and relationship counselling. They also provide psycho-sexual therapy. You must be over seventeen years of age.

The Gallery, Oxford Chambers, Oxford Place, Leeds, LS1
Telephone 0532 304747. Answerphone available.

SAFE HOUSE (THE CHILDREN'S SOCIETY)

Run away from home? Leeds has a safe house for run aways under the age of sixteen. Ring the number above for advice about emergency refuge provision. While you are at the safe house there will be someone to talk to about your problems.

Telephone 0532 304747

SAHARA (W)

Offers refuge for Black women and their children experiencing violence.

Telephone 0532 305087

SELF-HELP GROUPS (W)

Want to start your own self-help group? If you live in the Leeds area, try the City Council's Women's Committee. They might be able to help with running costs or perhaps with setting up a creche.

Contact Sandra McNeil 0532 474193
or regarding Women's Fund Grants
Beulah Mills 0532 474192
and about International Women's Day and Child Care grants.
Surji Cair 0532 474197

SHEFFIELD MALE SURVIVORS (M)

Telephone line only: 0742 796333

THE SURVIVORS' PROJECT (M)

Open Monday, Wednesday and Friday, 2.00 pm - 5.00 pm.
Do you feel the need to talk to other men who have been in a similar situation as yourself?
The Survivors' Project is a voluntary self-help project which provides information, advice and support for sexually abused men. It is Leeds and Wakefield based, and concentrates on West Yorkshire.
The project also runs closed groups which are confidential. New groups are formed every two or three months. The Survivors' Project can offer support for health checks, legal advice and help around your own

relationships. A female support worker is available if you prefer this. There is a twenty-four hour answerphone available.

Telephone 0532 350191

SHEFFIELD YOUTH CLINIC
Provides information and advice on sexual health and relationships. All young people are welcome. Ring 3.30 pm - 6.00 pm, Monday and Tuesday; 4.00 pm - 6.30 pm, Wednesday.

1 Mulberry Street, Civic Centre, Sheffield 1 2PJ
Telephone 0742 716790

VICTIM SUPPORT SCHEMES
Provides temporary refuge for women and their children who have suffered mental, sexual or physical harrassment/ violence. Phone for details, 9.15 am - 5.00 pm, Monday to Friday. Over the weekends there is an answerphone service or you can contact via the Social Services Emergency Duty Team and The Samaritans. Languages available: Urdu, Punjabi.
There is a drop-in service to provide help, support and advice to any woman threatened by violence (ring to check the hours).

Bradford: 0274 390876
Calderdale: 0422 344742
Huddersfield: 0484 51724
Keighley: 0535 606871
Leeds:
NE Leeds 0532 604646/7
NW Leeds 0532 461167
S and W Leeds 0532 713558
Wakefield 0924 369107

WOMEN'S AID and the WOMEN'S AID RESOURCE CENTRE (W)

P.O. Box 89, Wellington Street, Leeds LS1 2EE
Telephone 0532 460401 (Twenty four hour answerphone)

WOMEN'S COUNSELLING AND THERAPY SERVICE (W)
Do you need someone to talk to?
The Leeds Women's Counselling and Therapy Service offers a free and confidential drop-in session on Tuesdays 2.30 pm - 6.30 pm and Thursdays 10.00 am - 2.00 pm. A service for Black women is available on Fridays 10.00 am - 2.00 pm.
WCTS also offers psychodynamic psychotherapy - primarily a talking therapy. If you live in Leeds and are interested in using the service, contact the office and an interview will be arranged with one of the

therapists, usually within one month of contact. The purpose of this initial assessment is to come to a joint decision as to whether or not WCTS can help. It involves getting clear information about your life, discussing the type of therapy you might have and agreeing areas you want to work on. If the WCTS cannot offer you something suitable then they will try to suggest alternative sources of help.

Oxford Chambers, Oxford Place, Leeds LS13 3AX
Telephone 0532 455725 (Twenty-four hour answerphone)

WOMEN'S HEALTH MATTERS (W)
Provides information and advice on women's health concerns.

Room 8c Vassalli House, 20 Central Road, Leeds LS1 6DE
Telephone 0532 421070

WPF COUNSELLING NORTH
WPF seeks to help people who suffer from emotional, psychological and relational problems on a one-to-one basis. It aims to make counselling help available to all sections of the community and has a national network of local centres.

An initial interview is offered to prospective clients as soon as possible, to assess their particular difficulties. Then individual counselling is arranged weekly, on a one-to-one basis, with another counsellor. Group counselling is also available. Counselling can be short term, or on a longer term basis, depending on need. Every client pays something, but nobody is excluded because of a low income.

Leeds Bridge House, Third Floor, Hunslet Road, Leeds LS10 1JN
Telephone 0532 450303